Children's Parties

Children's Parties

Ideas, Planning, Cakes, Food, and Games.

Angela Hollest
and
Penelope Gaine

PIATKUS

To David, Edward and Clare,
and Michael, David and Daniel.

Authors' acknowledgement
We would like to thank Christine Curzon, who typed the manuscript
and struggled with our handwriting; Cetra Long, who so cleverly
visualized our ideas; all our friends who generously shared their
experiences with us – both the triumphs and the disasters; and our
families for their patience and willingness to try and test everything.

First published in 1983 by Judy Piatkus (Publishers) Limited
of Loughton, Essex

British Library Cataloguing in Publication Data

Hollest, Angela
   Children's parties.
   1. Children's parties
   I. Title   II. Gaine, Penelope
   793.2'1   GV1205
 ISBN 0–86188–401–9

Drawings by Cetra Long

Photography by John Lee and Anthea Sieveking

Design by Dave Allen

Typesetting by Wyvern Typesetting Ltd, Bristol
Printed and bound by The Garden City Press Limited,
Letchworth, Herts.

The publishers would like to thank Galt Toys of Muswell Hill, London N10,
and Party Place, 67 Gloucester Avenue, London NW1, for providing various
props for use in the photographs.

Contents

Introduction

We are not qualified cooks or entertainers, but we are, like you, qualified mothers! This book evolved because we found there was neither a realistic nor complete guide to the nerve-racking experience of giving a children's party. We decided, in between feeding the puppy, digging the veg patch and coping with the measles, to produce this reference book for others who may similarly have searched in vain.

This book is designed to give you plenty of scope to plan your style of party. The chapter on cakes includes simple designs, as well as more complicated ones – although all of them can be achieved without any particular culinary skill! The section on ice cream cakes is deliberately simple – there is little cooking – and similarly, the party food chapter is designed to allow you plenty of choice, showing you how to cater for your children's party as diversely and economically as possible. We have tried to produce the party planning and games chapters in a realistic way, so that you can choose how to organize your event according to your budget and time. And although this is basically a book for parties, you can also make use of the ideas just for a special tea, following, for example, a holiday outing to the zoo.

Above all, we want you to be able to adapt it to your own lifestyle. It's great if you have time to make your own invitations, but don't be disheartened if not – maybe next year you won't be coping with night feeds, or you could start planning a little earlier. Don't despair if that doesn't work, though – there is no stigma in not producing home-made invitations, food and presents. You can't do everything! But we hope that we have provided you with plenty of possibilities, so that at the end of the day you will have that special hug and be thanked for the best party ever!

1. TEA PARTY PLANNING

In this part of the book, there are ideas for making invitations, for decorations, for presents, and for party themes. We also have a section on fancy dress, directed particularly at non-sewers like us, which relies basically on making do with what is at hand, with only a few simple instructions for making the odd garment or hat. Our aim is to achieve easy but effective outfits.

Although we give you plenty of suggestions for everything, don't panic if you feel you can't cope: a few balloons can be quite enough decoration. All these ideas are for you to put into practice only if you have the time and energy. And indeed, if you share your party with a friend, you could each take a section on which to concentrate your time and skills – for instance, one of you could make decorations, and the other some fudge or other presents to take home.

First things first

First fix the date, numbers and venue of your party. If you are using a church or village hall, then you will have to organize this well ahead. Do check your facilities if using a venue other than your home. A friend organized a Christmas party for fifty under-fives in a local hall, with Father Christmas and all the trimmings; horror-struck, she sat up in bed the night before the party, realizing the function was to raise money to provide loos for the hall. . . . She managed with a row of potties behind a screen, and very little orange to drink for tea!

Make a list of the names of the children you are inviting to the party. If you are planning a joint effort with another mother make sure that you both know how many you are inviting. If your party is being held at home, limit the number of children to the capacity of the house (half a dozen seven-year-olds can seem like a herd of elephants) and to your capacity for coping. Even in a hall and sharing a party, don't be tempted to go mad with your numbers unless you have sufficient helpers.

Send your invitations out about three weeks to a fortnight before the date of the party. You can of course just telephone the mothers, but children do love to receive their own post, and have a written invitation especially for them. You can deliver them by hand, particularly to children attending the same school as yours. If you cannot manage to ask the whole class give them to the teacher, so that she can distribute

them discreetly. If your party is going to be held in the holidays, be sure you know all the children's names and addresses from school, so that you can contact them if your child develops mumps, and you need to cancel the party! Tick off the names of the children who have accepted, but be sufficiently flexible to allow enough room and food for the occasional child you thought wasn't coming, but turns up anyway.

When planning your party, above all else, have sufficient helpers to organize a trail of children needing to go to the loo after tea (don't let them lock the door), to hand out the coats, balloons and presents at the end, and generally to assist where necessary. You cannot run a party single-handed even when the children are older, so try to have two helpers, so that two of you can run the games while the third organizes tea.

A few simple rules will keep the party running smoothly and avoid confusion. We are great believers in lists – they make life so much easier.

1. Make a list of your guests (plus telephone numbers).

2. Have a list of the food you are planning and check that it is all on the table. We found some cheese straws sitting in a tin in solitary splendour several days after one party.

3. Make a detailed shopping list, including anything you are buying for the table – paper plates, napkins, etc – as well as balloons, prizes, going-home presents, and food.

4. Make a list of the games you intend the children to play, and check that all the equipment (eg, a parcel for Pass the Parcel) is organized. Make sure you have enough little prizes. If you are having musical games, check that you have a suitable record or tape, and that your helper knows how to work the machine. Don't be too proud to look at the games list halfway through the party if your mind goes blank.

5. If you are having an entertainer (see below) have ready a contingency plan of games in case he is late or fails to turn up. Be prepared for the worst and it will never happen.

6. Do not have any open fires, even with very satisfactory guards. Accidents do happen, particularly with flimsy party dresses, in the general excitement. Use electric blow heaters if you need extra heat quickly.

7. Have a simple first aid kit available in case of need (always keep Waspeze to hand for summer outdoor parties).

8. Have your camera, film and flash light ready and working.

9. Don't forget a box of matches for the cake candles.

Escape routes

We do not suggest that you have entertainers for very young children. The children have to be at an age when they can concentrate sufficiently to enjoy and appreciate the treat, and not get restless and fidget. Older children, from five upwards, love having entertainment of some sort at their parties, but this does not mean they do not want games as well. So time your party to have warm-up games before tea, tea itself, the entertainment and

more games at the end of the party. We feel that three-quarters of an hour is sufficient time for the entertainer for five- to seven-year-olds, but after that the shows can last for an hour or more.

It is best to have entertainers recommended by friends and acquaintances, but if you look in your local newspaper advertisements and in the Yellow Pages, you can find several alternatives for entertainment: a film show, a magician, a balloon man, or a Punch and Judy (our man once swallowed Punch's voice whistle!). Some entertainers take over the entire party, and all you do is provide tea, which they even help to serve – what a doddle!

Whoever you use, you will need to book them early. Some need four to five months' advance booking, especially if you are planning a party at a weekend, a bank holiday or Christmas. It is also very important to check whether or not they have done any shows in your area, and with a similar age group to the one for which you are catering. They can alter their programme accordingly. Always check, if having a film show, exactly which films you will be getting. Don't forget to write and confirm the booking, and if there is any doubt, enclose a set of clear instructions of how to find your home. There is nothing worse than the feeling of panic that creeps over one while waiting for the 'pièce de résistance' of the party to make an entry, and trying to organize extra games to occupy restless and expectant children! We have both had this experience, and both times the excuse was that the entertainer had got lost. The other result of a later start to the show is that you will have parents arriving at the given time to collect children and you may have to entertain *them* for longer than anticipated, unless they can squeeze in and watch the show too. (At all

times have this book to hand to whisk up some impromptu games for the children or liquid refreshments for the adults!)

When booking the entertainer, check how long his programme will last. You can then organize what time to serve tea, remembering to leave enough time to ferry everyone to the loo before they sit down for the treat. Despite this efficiency, you will find some children will need to get up in the middle of the show, so when arranging seating leave sufficient space for them to squeeze out comparatively easily and quietly. Also remember that your guests will fidget least if they are 'sitting comfortably'. Even if you haven't enough chairs, put cushions, rugs or pillows on the floor for them to sit on. If you are having a long film for older and less messy children, why not hand out a small packet of crisps or Monster Munch, etc, for each child, half way through – although think twice about this if they are sitting on your beautifully upholstered chairs.

Always remember, when planning to have an entertainer, to be practical. It is not easy to have to remove the remains of tea, tables, chairs, etc, to make way for the conjuror's equipment. You really need to have separate rooms for tea and the show, especially as nearly all entertainers want to set up their props beforehand.

If you are using your own video, and hiring a film to show, again remember to check the time the film will last. Also do not invite more guests to this sort of party than can comfortably sit and watch a small television screen.

Entertainers are not cheap. They are extremely popular, but don't worry if you cannot afford to employ one. So long as you have sufficient games organized, the children will be just as happy.

Party themes

If you like the idea of giving a party with a special theme linking all the different elements in the party, then here are lots of ideas for you – games, decorations, cake, take-home presents, and so on. You may decide to give a fancy dress party, inviting all the children to come as pirates or as nursery rhyme characters; or you could give a simpler kind of fancy dress party – a kings and queens party, for instance, where the children only need a cloak and a crown, and their usual clothes underneath – or a hat party which is self-explanatory. The fancy dress section at the end of this chapter is very simple and involves very little sewing. The most important thing is that the children must be happy in their outfits or they will be uncomfortable for the whole party.

Keep your party simple – use our ideas as a basis, but don't feel you have to do everything we suggest: adapt them to suit you, your child and your own lifestyle. A party is meant to be fun and not all hard work.

Teddy Bear's Picnic

If the weather is good enough have the party outside (if you are only having a few children then a picnic in the countryside or in a park would be more exciting.) Make teddy bear invitations, invite teddies too. Use Winnie the Pooh wrapping paper, tea towels, etc, to decorate the room or house if the party is indoors. Make a teddy bear cake or ice cream cake. Sit teddy bears on the table and label, 'Paddington's marmalade sandwiches' and 'Pooh's honey treats' for the children's sandwiches. Pin the nose on the Teddy and have a suitable mini Paddington or Pooh prize in the Pass the Parcel game.

Army Party

You could use this theme if you are giving your child an Action Man, a fort or a tank as his birthday present. The cake could be the castle or the tank, as well. Decorate the table with toy soldiers, and give one to each boy as a going-home present. The boys could come dressed as soldiers. Use the assault course in the summer (see the games section).

Space Age Party

This theme would be ideal if you are giving your child a space rocket or space Lego for a present. Make the space ship invitations and the space ship cake. Decorate the room with *Star Wars* or space ship posters, record sleeves, or whatever you have. Use silver foil to decorate the table.

Cowboy and Indian Party

Ask the children to come as cowboys and Indians. Divide the guests into two teams – one cowboys and one Indians – for games, going into tea and so on. This theme would go well if you are giving your child a fort, a cowboy outfit or wigwam. Make the cowboy and Indian cake and use more plastic cowboys and

Indians to decorate the table. Use them as prizes and play Pinning the tail on the Bronco, and Shoeing the Horse etc.

Motor Party

Give your son a garage or a lorry as a present. Make a motor racing cake, a car cake or a garage cake. Have toy cars on the tea table. Put a toy car in the centre of the pass-the-parcel as the prize. (If you do put cars on the table, then be prepared for spills!)

Clock Party

This could be combined with giving your child a toy clock to help him learn the time, or a real child's clock or watch. Make clock invitations, and make the clock cake. Give toy watches as prizes or going-home presents. If it's a party for tiny children, start off with, What's the time, Mr Wolf?

Riding Party

Very popular with little girls! If you are lucky you might be able to borrow a pony (good tempered) for pony rides (in which case, remember to specify jeans or riding clothes on the invitations). Make sure you have efficient help. Give your child a present relevant to riding – a riding hat, jodphurs or a crop. Make a gymkhana cake. Decorate the room with horsy posters and rosettes, if you have any. You could play Pin the Tail on the Pony (*not* the real one) as one of the games.

Football Party

Make football invitations. Ask the boys to come dressed as footballers. Hang up a pair of boots on the front door instead of balloons. Cut up old football magazines and put up as decorations. Use the colours and rosettes of your son's favourite soccer team to decorate the table. Make the football match cake. Have a football game, out of doors, if you have room. In any case, divide the children into two teams for playing games, and give each child the name of a famous footballer – you could have the name and a photograph of him on a piece of card to pin to the child's jumper. Wrap the going-home presents in the colours of your son's favourite football team.

Pirate Party

Make the skull and crossbone invitations. You could decorate the room with cutlasses (cut out of card and covered in foil) or skulls and crossbones. Have one on the front door, instead of balloons. Make the galleon cake for tea. Play pirate games like Musical Islands (with cushions), Pin the treasure on the Island, with a big picture of an island (like Pinning the tail on the Donkey), and have a treasure hunt. Give chocolate money in gold foil as prizes. Also have a big box of treasure trove from which to dispense the presents at the end of the party.

Farm Party

If you are giving your child a model farm, or tractor as his main birthday present, then why not make this the theme of the party? Make a tractor cake, put little farm animals on the table and give these to the children, as their going-home presents. If your son has toy tractors have them down the centre of the table, as decoration (but don't be surprised if the children play around with them). Play farm games – The Farmer's in his Den, Old Macdonald had a Farm, and so on.

Noah's Ark Party

Ask the guests to come as animals. Use an animal template, or stencil, for the invitations. Pair the children off for games and for going in to tea two by two. Make a Noah's Ark cake for tea, and animal biscuits. Put plastic animals on the table, two by two if you wish. If you can find any suitable posters, or magazine pictures, you could Blu-tack them to the walls, or make concertina cut-outs of animals and attach them around the room, and on the doors. Stick little animals on their bags for presents. Play animal orientated games – the Tail on the donkey game, What's the time, Mr Wolf?, and so on. If you have anything that looks like a Noah's Ark, use it for the going-home presents if it's large enough. You could make animal felt finger puppets (see page 37) for going-home presents.

Zoo Party

This would be fun if you were taking children to the zoo for a treat first. Make a zoo cake for tea, and see Noah's Ark party, above, for other ideas.

Hallowe'en or Witches and Wizards Party

Ask the guests to come as witches or wizards – this only needs a hat and cloak. Make witch or wizard invitations. Decorate the room with hollowed-out pumpkins with holes for eyes and mouth. Put night lights in them, but keep them well out of harm's way. If you can't get hold of pumpkins, put nightlights in jam jars and sellotape coloured tissue paper around the *outside* of the jar. Again, keep them well out of reach. Hang up moons and stars cut out of foil, or fasten them to the walls. You could replace your ordinary light bulbs with blue or red ones, which is particularly effective at tea time. Play Apple Bobbing, and make a witch cake for tea, and toffee apples for the children to take home.

Firework Party

You can either let off your own fireworks, or go to a local firework display first, and bring the children back to tea. Send rocket cards for the invitations. If you are having your own firework party at home, then remember to keep the children well back from the fireworks. Very small children may be frightened so let them watch from indoors. Always have plenty of adult helpers. Make a rocket cake for tea and lots of sausages.

Easter Party

Send egg-shaped invitation cards. Have an Easter egg hunt as one of the games. Decorate the table with chocolate Easter eggs, or decorated hard-boiled eggs and with Easter chicks. You could give the eggs and the chicks and egg cosies (see page 38) to the guests to take home. Make a Humpty Dumpty cake, or an Easter nest cake for tea.

Hat Party

Make hat invitations, and ask all the children to come in a special hat, for instance: top hat, bowler, cap, riding hat, cowboy hat, Indian feathers, crown, saucepan hat, scarecrow hat, witch's hat, medieval lady's hat, straw hat, poke bonnet, chef's hat, hat with a salad on it, flower hat, etc, etc. Play Musical Hats with them all!

Kings and Queens Party

Send out invitations in the shape of crowns, using gold card if you can. Ask the guests to come as kings and queens (they only need a cloak and crown). Decorate the room and the tea table with crowns cut out of foil, and red crepe paper cut into strips. If you like, you could use red crepe paper to cover the table and staple crowns to it. Use red paper napkins. Games to play: Treasure Hunt, Oranges and Lemons, Musical Crowns. Make the castle cake for tea, and if you can find a model king and queen put them on their castle cake. Give red balloons and gold chocolate money as going-home presents.

Nursery Rhyme Party

Stencil a nursery rhyme figure for the invitations, and ask the guests to come as a nursery rhyme character. Decorate the room with nursery rhyme wrapping paper fastened to the walls. You can also cover the table with it if you like. For tea you could make either a Humpty Dumpty cake, a farm cake or a Little Bo Peep cake (make the doll cake on page 62 and add a shepherd's crook made out of a pipe cleaner, and some little lambs). Give the children little nursery rhyme books to take home.

Seasonal Party

If your child's birthday falls at an inconvenient time, or if you are working, consider giving a Christmas, Easter or Summer holiday party instead.

Wurzel Gummidge and Aunt Sally Party

Ask the children to dress up as Wurzels and Aunt Sallys. Make a farm cake for tea, and put a plastic scarecrow on it. Make a simple scarecrow with a broom handle securely fixed in sand or earth in a large pot, and a bamboo cane tied horizontally: dress him in old clothes, and hang the going-home presents from his arms. If the party is in the garden, tuck straw into his clothes; if indoors, stand him in the corner of the room, and forget the straw!

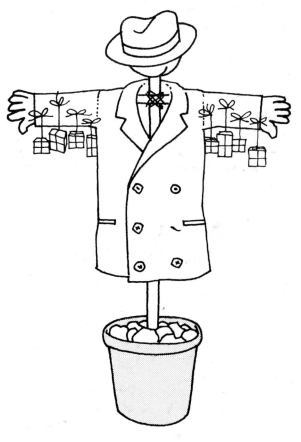

Party Invitations

Some very attractive invitations can be bought, but they are not at all difficult to make, and are great fun to do, although they take time. Try and involve the children in making their own invitations, but remember that until they are about seven years old their help will be more enthusiastic than practical. Make the wording of the invitation absolutely clear. It is very easy to forget a vital ingredient, such as the date of the party or address! Use your own wording but check that you include all the details given on the right:

LAURA invites DANIEL to come to her
BIRTHDAY PARTY
On 2 April
From 4 pm to 6 pm

At   RSVP
12, Princes Drive,   *or*
Blenheim   Please answer

If you are having the party in the garden or after school, put 'garden' or 'school' clothes. There is nothing worse than arriving in a long dress when everyone else is in wellington boots. If you have decided to give a fancy dress party or one with a particular theme – pirates, scarecrows, nursery rhymes, etc – then put this on the invitation as well.

When making your own invitations, in order to avoid a happy fun idea getting into a muddle and causing frayed tempers, decide on your design in advance. Assemble your materials on the kitchen table, or on any other large flat surface that won't get damaged by paint, scissors, and so on, and organize your children into helping sensibly as far as they are able, colouring the cards, for instance. Don't be disappointed if your child is not the constructive type, or if you find he/she simply cannot concentrate for long enough. Be prepared to do nearly all the work and let your child have all the credit!

For all the ideas below, you will need some fairly stiff coloured card, coloured felt pens, sharp scissors, ruler, and envelopes to fit the finished cards. The invitations here are designed to fit p.o.p. (Post Office preferred) envelopes $4\frac{1}{2} \times 6\frac{1}{2}''$ (11·5 × 16·5 cm). If you are coordinating the party to follow a specific theme this can be introduced at the invitation stage.

Cut-out Invitations

For the simplest invitation, cut the shapes from single card, and write the details on the back and front of the shape.

Trace the outline of one of the drawings we include here and on the next two pages, of a gingerbread man, a flower, balloons, cat, space rocket and clown. If these don't fit your theme, draw for yourself a clock (with hands pointing to party time or child's age), ship, crown, teddy bear, etc. Keep the outline bold and simple and make sure there is plenty of space for all the party details.

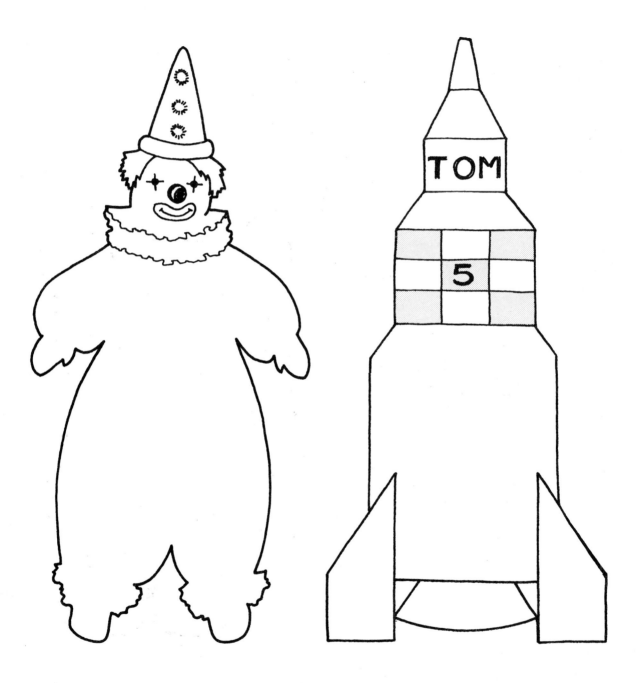

Folded Invitations

Another kind of card is one that is folded in half, and stands up on its own. Decide on the finished size of your invitations, making sure they fit your envelopes. Measure out the coloured card, fold the card in half, and cut it out very neatly. You could use pinking shears for an attractive zig-zag edge. Trace or draw your design, and decorate the front by colouring it or using a stick of glue (Pritt Stick) to make a pattern and then shaking glitter over it (allow time for the glue to dry before shaking off the glitter). Use the inside of the card to write all the details of the invitation.

Try one of these designs on the front of your folded card: skull and crossbones, Easter egg. Alternatively, you could draw for yourself a birthday cake, football, crown, wrapped present, cracker, and so on, or adapt a drawing from one of the other sections, adding more detail and colour or glitter.

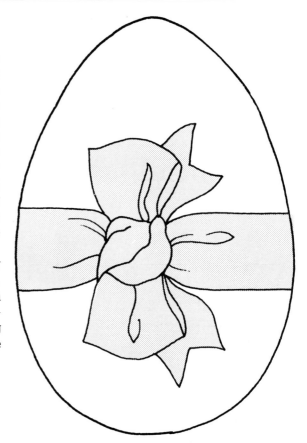

Concertina Cards

A more interesting and slightly more complicated invitation is a concertina card. Decide on the size of the finished invitations. Multiply the width by four, measure with a ruler and cut it out. Mark out four widths with little pencil marks top and bottom and fold them as shown. Draw a shape on the top layer and cut round it through all the layers, remembering to leave a join on each side. Colour all layers and write the invitation on the inside. The elephant, house and Christmas tree look very effective, or you could experiment with your own designs.

Mask Invitations

If you are having a fancy dress party, send mask invitations. Cut out a piece of coloured card to shape. Pierce two holes either side and put on a hole reinforcer on each one. Thread through two pieces of string or

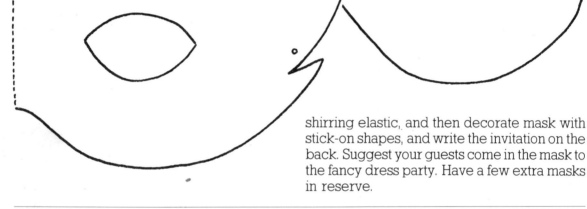

shirring elastic, and then decorate mask with stick-on shapes, and write the invitation on the back. Suggest your guests come in the mask to the fancy dress party. Have a few extra masks in reserve.

Fancy dress costumes

The majority of the costumes listed are simply made from old shirts, dresses, pieces of material etc. – and most of them require no sewing at all. Accessories are often found in the toy cupboard, or can be put together with a little imagination, occasionally with a little glue. There are ideas for boys and for girls.

Cowboy

A cowboy hat and plenty of guns. If your cowboy is still quite little let him ride a hobby horse. Spotted handkerchief to tie around his neck. A check or gingham shirt. A pair of jeans tucked into wellington boots to look more like cowboy boots. Sheriff's badge.

Coalman

Cap (black) with peak turned back to front. Old shirt. Long trousers with string tied round just below the knee. A pair of wellington boots. Plenty of black face paint and, if possible, a sack (not too dirty!).

Ghost

One small sheet (depending on the size of your child). Cover the child with the sheet and mark on the centre with a pencil, very carefully, where the eyes come, then remove the sheet and cut out the eye holes. Sew some elastic to fit your child's head by the side of each eye so that it goes around the back of the head, to hold the sheet in place. If you have any old black net, you could tack this over the top of the sheet to give an eerie cloud effect.

Soldier

You can purchase camouflage outfits. If you have one of these send your child with a rifle and his face blacked in non-toxic face paints. You can assemble your own camouflage or similar army kit if you have an army jersey (with elbow and shoulder patches), a pair of green or brown trousers and a green beret.

Wee Willie Winkie

If you do not have a suitable night gown, then one of Dad's old collarless shirts (or one of your own!) might be suitable. Some sort of a nightcap – perhaps you have a suitable bobble hat, which could be made to look like a nightcap – and a candle and candle holder.

Surgeon or Doctor

A man's white collarless shirt, worn back to front, or a painting overall. A white face mask. A pair of wellington boots. A doctor's kit. Make the face mask out of a piece of muslin or thin cotton. Sew two lengths of tape on either side so that the mask can be worn over the nose and mouth. If he has a doctor's kit then put the stethoscope around his neck.

Chef

White jeans, man's white collarless shirt as tunic over trousers. Catch waist with belt and tuck a white napkin into this. Chef's hat (see diagram). If you have a stripy butcher's apron, he could wear that. If you have a meat tenderizer, let him take this but *never* let your child carry a knife of any sort. Or he could carry a tray full of buns he has 'just baked'!

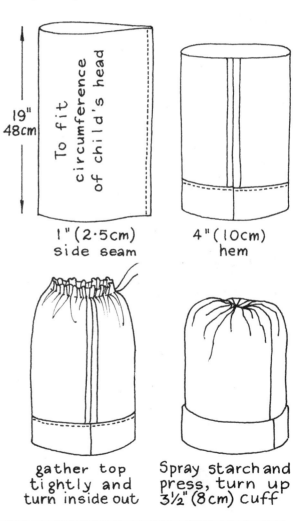

19" 48cm

To fit circumference of child's head

1" (2.5cm) side seam

4" (10cm) hem

gather top tightly and turn inside out

Spray starch and press, turn up 3½" (8cm) cuff

Straw hat tied with ribbon

Rosebud mouth, lashes drawn on lids, circles of blusher on cheeks

Pretty dress and lace petticoats

White tights

Black shoes

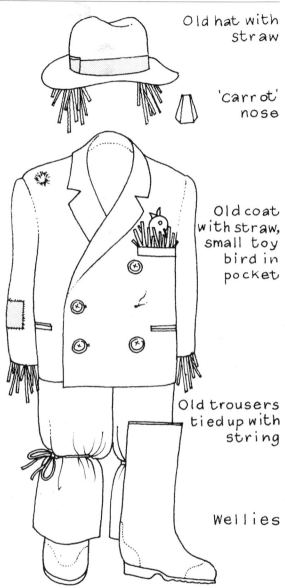

Old hat with straw

'carrot' nose

Old coat with straw, small toy bird in pocket

Old trousers tied up with string

Wellies

Aunt Sally

Follow the drawing to create this very easy but attractive costume. Finish off with round red cheeks, made-up eyes and heart-shaped lips.

Wurzel Gummidge

The drawing shows details of this costume. You will need to stitch the straw (or raffia) to the jacket and the hat. Cut the nose (right) out of carrot-coloured card, and glue flaps.

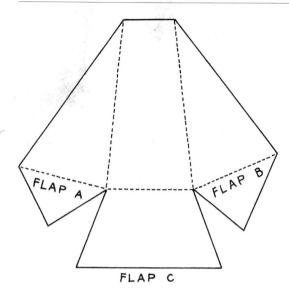

FLAP A   FLAP B

FLAP C

Fold along dotted lines and glue
Flap A and Flap B to Flap C.

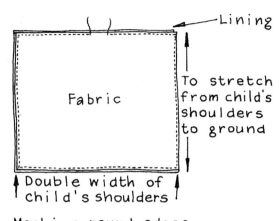

Lining

Fabric

To stretch
from child's
shoulders
to ground

Double width of
child's shoulders

Machine round edges
leaving opening, turn
inside out and press

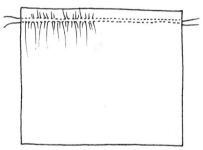

Sew 2 rows gathering
Pull up to fit

Attach neck band
and ties

King or Queen

Measure your child's head and make a suitably-sized crown out of card. Cover the crown with silver foil by stapling it, or by gluing it to the inside of the crown. Decorate by spreading glue on the tips and edge of the crown and sprinkle glitter over it. Leave to dry and shake off extra glitter. Glue on cotton wool ermine and contrasting coloured-foil jewels.

Use a plain coloured dressing gown as the king's robe, and fasten an old gilt chain round his neck, and a gold belt round his middle. Or make this simple cloak (see right), in red or purple, with a tie fastening. You can dress up his shoes with a bobble of fur or some jewels, stick a sword in his belt, and make an orb or sceptre for him to carry.

You will need a long party dress or pretty night dress for your Queen, and give her a full-length cloak and glittering jewellery.

Footballer

Football shorts, football shirt, football boots, football socks, and football, will probably be your son's favourite outfit, particularly if you can organize this in the colour of his favourite team.

Robin Hood

Green tunic (see page 30) with shirt. If your child does not object you could also put him into some green tights. Stick a feather in the side of a suitable hat. Make the hat out of green felt (see diagram). A bow and arrow to carry.

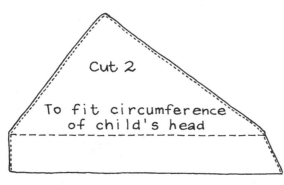

Cut 2

To fit circumference of child's head

Sew sides and crown
Turn inside out

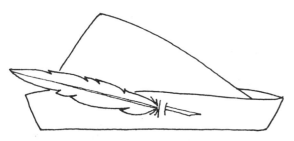

Fold up brim along dotted line, attach feather

Christopher Robin

Ideal for a shy boy as basically there is no dressing up! Summer: white sunhat, wellingtons, shorts and shirt, and a teddy to carry. Winter: sou'wester and matching mackintosh, wellingtons and a teddy.

Clown

There are endless possibilities here. Make a fat clown by putting a cushion inside large pyjamas with braces to keep them up. Use a stuffed pair of large shoes but let your child take ordinary shoes for wearing after the fancy dress parade as he might trip over. Hat with droopy paper flowers. Sew patches onto clothes. Use face paints to make either a sad or happy clown or make one side of his face smiling and one crying.

Paddington Bear

A suitable man's hat (it doesn't matter if it's rather large); a duffle coat (the longer the better), a pair of corduroy trousers, and wellington boots. A luggage label with the usual message 'Please look after this bear'. He will need a small suitcase to carry, and a marmalade sandwich if you can trust him! Put suitable labels on the suitcase too.

Highwayman

Make a mask (see page 22) and dress him in cowboy hat, black trousers, black cape (see cloak, page 25) or use an old curtain, black polo-neck jumper and black gumboots. Let him ride a hobby horse, if you have one. Give him some old jewellery in a jewel case or little sack for his booty, and a couple of pistols to carry.

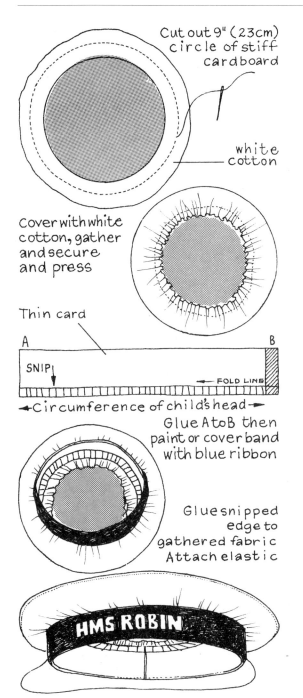

Cut out 9" (23cm) circle of stiff cardboard

white cotton

Cover with white cotton, gather and secure and press

Thin card

A   B

SNIP ↓   FOLD LINE →

←Circumference of child's head→

Glue A to B then paint or cover band with blue ribbon

Glue snipped edge to gathered fabric Attach elastic

HMS ROBIN

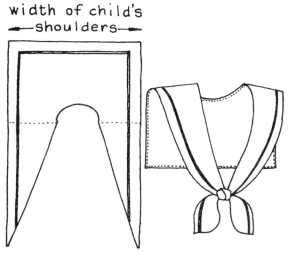

width of child's
→ shoulders ←

White cotton, hemmed, with blue trimming

Sailor

Blue and white striped T-shirt, and blue trousers. Make a collar and a hat (see diagrams). He should carry a toy telescope.

Dick Whittington

A toy cat. A man's shirt belted at the waist, tights, wellington boots, and large red and white spotted hanky tied into a bag round a stick – for his traditional bundle of possessions. Optional hat (see Robin Hood's hat, page 26).

Birds

One long-sleeved polo-neck jumper, or brown long-sleeved T-shirt. Brown woollen balaclava, if you have one, with a beak (see next page) stapled on to the front. Brown, yellow or black tights. Dancing shoes, plimsolls or brown sandals. Brown wings attached to the child's wrists and back (see Fairy's

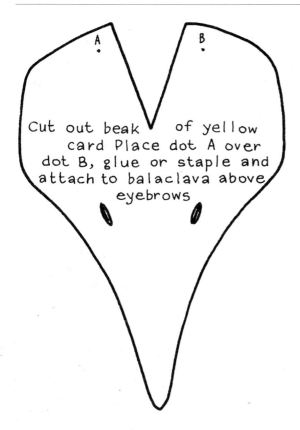

Cut out beak of yellow
card Place dot A over
dot B, glue or staple and
attach to balaclava above
eyebrows

Animals

Use a similar basic outfit as for the birds. Make felt ears for a rabbit (see diagrams on how to make these). Use a puff of cotton wool for his tail. For a donkey (Eeyore) make the outfit in grey or brown with long ears and a donkey's tail with a red bow on it. Make the tail out of a brown stocking or half a pair of tights stuffed and sewn on to the child's tights. For a cat, black tights, polo neck and balaclava (see diagram for pussy cat ears). Stuff a black stocking as above for the tail. Use face paints to draw whiskers on face.

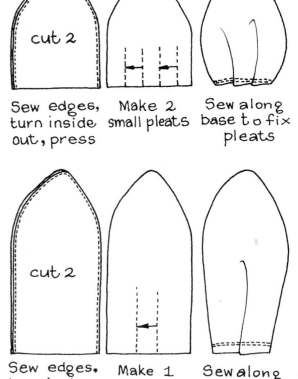

cut 2

Sew edges, turn inside out, press

Make 2 small pleats

Sew along base to fix pleats

cut 2

Sew edges, turn inside out, press

Make 1 small pleat

Sew along base to fix pleats

wings on page 30 for detailed instructions). You could staple pieces of overlapping feather-shaped paper to the material. For the tail, if you can get hold of some pheasant feathers (ask your butcher) make an arrangement of these, and carefully sew them on to the back of the tights, at waist height (remind the child to be careful when he sits down).

You could also have a completely black outfit, for a blackbird, or a completely white outfit, for a swan. For an owl use a cloak or curtain (see page 25) as a base and staple paper feather shapes to it. Attach two clusters of feathers to the balaclava for the owl's ears. Use brown face paints, and leave a large circle of white round each eye.

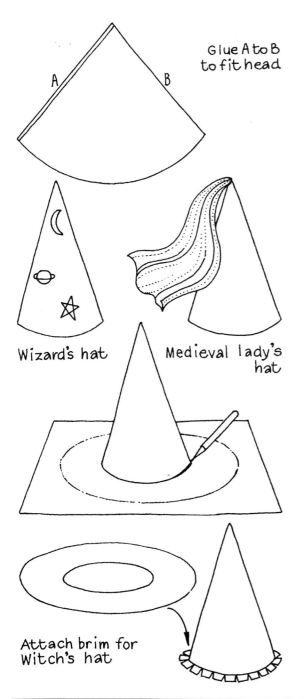

Glue A to B to fit head

Wizard's hat

Medieval lady's hat

Attach brim for Witch's hat

Sorcerer or Wizard

A long dressing gown or cloak (page 25). A witch's hat cut out from coloured paper, covered with stars and moons made out of foil (see diagram). Make some more to attach to the dressing gown or cloak. Give him a wand (see fairy's wand diagram), and a very fat book labelled spells.

Fine Lady from Banbury Cross

Cover a medieval style hat (see left) with foil. A light piece of net or nylon (part of an old lacy petticoat) could be attached to flow from the top of the cone. Secure the hat by a band of elastic stapled inside the cone to go under the chin. A long dress or pretty nightie will look most suitable, together with a cloak (see page 25). If you can manage it give her plenty of rings and jewellery and if you have any little bells attach these to the front of her shoes. You can buy lovely sounding bells which children use to play in a band, for her to hold. She could ride a hobby horse, if you have one.

Japanese Girl

You will need a suitable robe – a dressing gown, for instance. Make a cummerbund out of a wide piece of brightly coloured material. Wrap the cummerbund around the waist, and tie firmly at the back with a big bow. If your child has long hair, make the most of this by putting it into a bun, and use two coloured plastic knitting needles as long hair pins, sticking out of the bun. If your child has got short hair, you can make a bun from wool. Make up her face with white face paint, and give her slanting eyes, and red lips.

Tinkerbell or Fairy

Follow the drawings to make the separate items for this costume. If your daughter has a tutu let her wear this, instead of the tunic. Dancing shoes, if she has them. Make a flower hat in coloured tissue or crepe paper to match the dress.

To make the wings, you will need a piece of net or light material of the same colour as the dress. For the wand you need a piece of stick or a dowel rod 18″ (45 cm) long. Follow the diagram and then cover the corner staples with little pieces of tinsel sellotaped to the foil. Then take a long piece of tinsel and twist it around the rod, and secure firmly. If you want, you can add tinsel to her shoes and around the elastic bracelets. Cut out a little silver-foil bell, if you do not have one, for her to hold in her other hand as Tinkerbell.

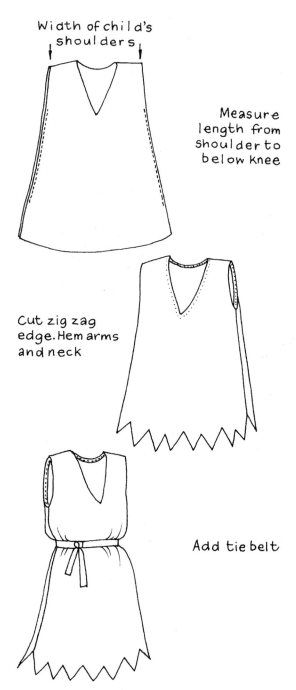

Width of child's shoulders

Measure length from shoulder to below knee

Cut zig zag edge. Hem arms and neck

Add tie belt

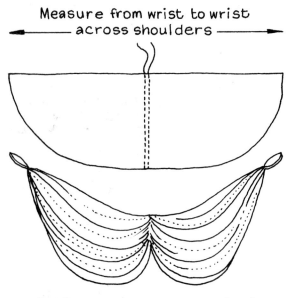

Measure from wrist to wrist across shoulders

Gather centre and sew to back of dress. Attach elastic loops to fit wrists

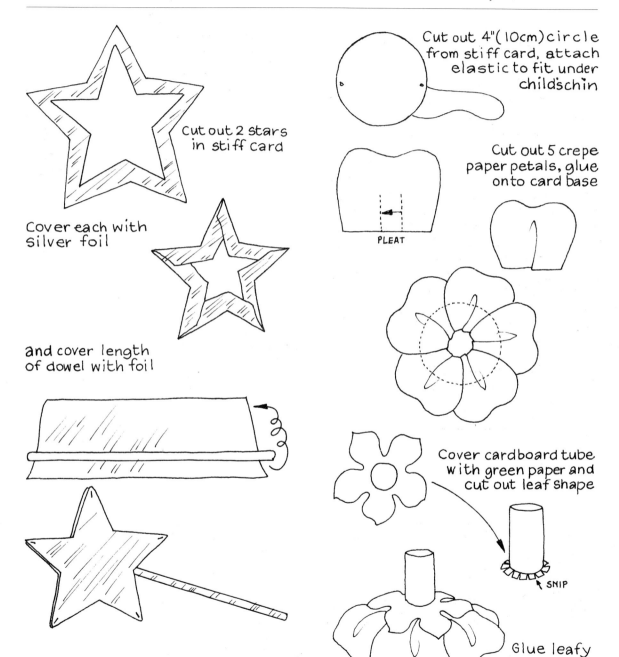

Cut out 2 stars in stiff card

Cover each with silver foil

and cover length of dowel with foil

Glue stars together over dowel, staple points

Cut out 4"(10cm) circle from stiff card, attach elastic to fit under child's chin

Cut out 5 crepe paper petals, glue onto card base

PLEAT

Cover cardboard tube with green paper and cut out leaf shape

SNIP

Glue leafy stalk to petal flower

Right: A pirates' tea party in full swing.

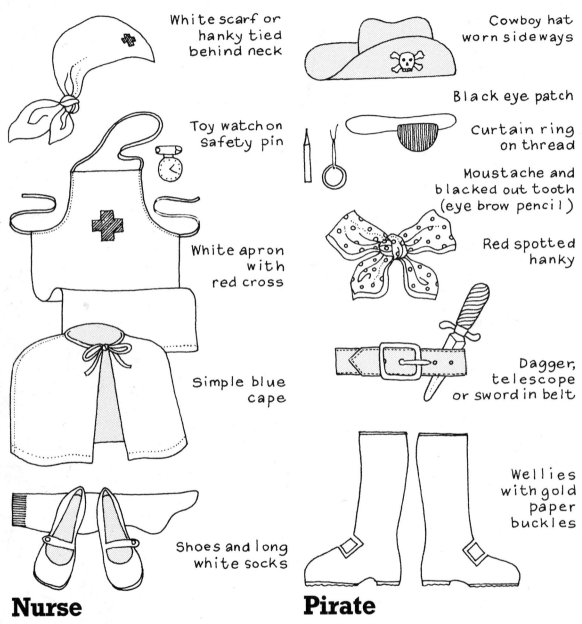

White scarf or hanky tied behind neck

Cowboy hat worn sideways

Black eye patch

Toy watch on safety pin

Curtain ring on thread

Moustache and blacked out tooth (eye brow pencil)

White apron with red cross

Red spotted hanky

Simple blue cape

Dagger, telescope or sword in belt

Wellies with gold paper buckles

Shoes and long white socks

Nurse

A blue and white cotton dress, either striped or checked, in other words a typical summer uniform dress, is the basis for this outfit which is shown in the drawing.

Pirate

The drawing shows everything you will need for this outfit. Start off by dressing him in a brightly coloured T-shirt and jeans and wellington boots.

Little Bo Peep

Dress your daughter in a pretty nightie. Give her a walking stick as a crook, wound with pink and white crepe paper, tied at the top with a bow. Secure the paper with sticky tape at the bottom and top, and fasten some small flowers and add lots of bows at the top. Make a mob cap (see diagram) or use a pretty bath hat. Give her a woolly lamb to carry.

Mary Mary Quite Contrary

A pretty nightie. A child's watering can, decorated with ribbons on the handle, tied in a bow. If you have any bells left over from Christmas, you could sew these if they are small enough, on to a hair band. Attach them also to the ribbon around the watering can, and make little wrist bands. Or make a mob cap, or use a pretty bath hat (see Little Bo Peep above).

Little Miss Muffet

Little Miss Muffet should really carry a toy spider, a bowl and spoon. Either make the spider out of pipe cleaners, dyed black with black ink or buy a horrid black plastic one. Attach a piece of cotton or thin elastic to the spider and tie this around your little girl's wrist. Put her in a nightie, with a mob cap (see above) and give her a bowl and spoon, for her curds and whey.

Waitress

Black tights, black skirt, white blouse, and little pinny and cap. Tray with plastic utensils on it.

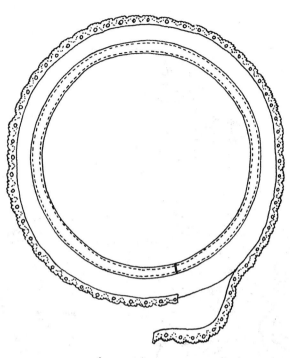

Cut out 28" (71cm) diameter circle of fabric, trim with lace and attach a wide bias binding channel 4" (10cm) from outside edge

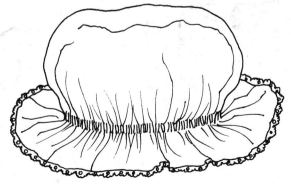

Insert elastic and pull up to fit child's head

Rider

This is a good outfit if your daughter already has riding gear. You could send her as a famous rider. You could put a number on a piece of card and tie it around her middle with a piece of string, as if she is competing in a show. If she has a riding crop she could carry that, or if she is young enough she could ride a hobby horse. If you have a rosette attach this to her horse!

Little Red Riding Hood

Make a red cloak and hood as in the drawing. Pretty little red or white dress to wear underneath, with an apron. A wicker basket with a gingham (red and white if possible) napkin over the top.

Cinderella

She could either be Cinderella going to the ball or Cinders. If Cinderella, she will need a pretty long dress or nightie, decorated with jewellery or tinsel and a little crown (see instructions for King's crown, page 25, but make it smaller to sit just on top of her head and staple elastic to either side to go under her chin). Decorate her shoes with tinsel and make her a foil clock face with the hands set at 12 o'clock to carry, or perhaps a small pumpkin.

If she is going as Cinders then blacken her face and give her really tatty clothes to wear. Cut or tear an old dress into spikes around the hem. Let her carry a besom broom (see opposite page).

For the Ugly Sisters, see page 36.

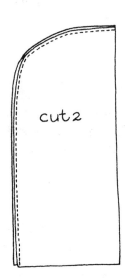

cut 2

Wrong sides together, sew back seam

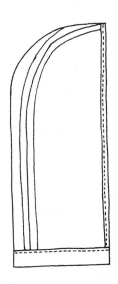

Hem all edges

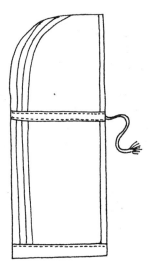

Attach wide bias binding, insert cord

Pull up cords and tie at neck

Alice in Wonderland

This is most suitable for a fair haired child. You will need a blue alice band, a blue and white striped dress (a similar school uniform dress would be fine), a white apron, a pair of white tights or long white socks. A plastic bottle with a label marked 'Drink me'.

Ballet Dancer

Use a tutu and ballet shoes, if you have them, and thin tights. If not, she could wear a leotard and leg warmers. If her hair is long, draw it back into a bun.

Witch

A black T-shirt, and long black skirt. Make the skirt by simply buying some very cheap black material and turning one end up to use as the waistline with elastic, and just join up the seams. If you have any black net, this is ideal for a cape to tack on to her shoulders, or make a simple black cloak (see page 25). A friend once even strung some old chop bones (scrubbed meticulously clean) to make a ghoulish necklace. Green nail varnish. A white powdered face, use child's talcum powder, or white face paints. Suitable eye make-up, and a couple of teeth blacked out. Strands of black wool sewn or stapled to the rim of a conical hat (see drawing on page 29) from underneath, and hanging down as hair.

If you have a suitably short broom handle, make it into a besom, by collecting some twigs, and firmly tying these with string to the broom handle. If you have a soft black toy cat she could take this under one arm, or attach it to the besom. An old book could be used as a book of spells.

Punk Rocker

Mini skirt or whatever 'with-it' gear you have! Washable coloured hair spray. Packet of glitter, packet of stars. (You can buy in chemists a special gel for sticking these on.) Coloured nail varnish. Bright face paint (non toxic) make-up. Sprinkle glitter in hair and on face, and decorate both with stars etc. Your child will enlighten you anyway as to the current trend!

Gipsy

Gold gipsy earrings, or brass curtain rings. Pretty frilly blouse, and pretty flower patterned skirt. Plenty of satin ribbons tied in bows, at the sleeves of the blouse and on either side of a hair band. An old lacy shawl. Black ballet shoes, or black canvas gym or tennis shoes. A tambourine if you have one, with satin ribbons as streamers.

Double Acts

If two of your children, or your child and a friend, are going to the same fancy dress party, then why not dress them up as a double act? Some of our suggestions are for boys and girls, but some could be either two boys or two girls.

Jack and Jill

Jack could be dressed in fairly traditional clothes, such as dungarees. Put brown paper as bandages around his head, and let him carry a large bottle labelled vinegar. Jill could wear a simple striped dress, or a long dress or nightie, with a pretty bow around her waist. Give her a bucket to carry. Decorate it with bows on the handle to make it look attractive.

Doctor and Patient

Doctor as on page 23. To make a patient, put him/her in pyjamas, dressing gown and slippers. Cut up an old sheet and bandage his head, one leg and arm and make a sling for his arm. If you have a walking stick let him use this.

Queen and Knave of Hearts

Dress the girl up as a queen (see page 25), and staple or tack lots of red paper hearts to the costume. Make some jam tarts and put them on an open tin or little tray (not to be eaten straight away). The Knave can wear either a man's shirt or one of yours, particularly if it has full sleeves, decorated with paper hearts. Belt it in at the waist. Or make a cardboard 'tabard' with shoulder and waist ties. Cover with foil and decorate with red paper hearts. Wear a red T-shirt underneath. Tights if he will wear them (if not, trousers).

Owl and Pussy Cat

See page 28. Let them carry between them a jar marked honey, lots of toy Monopoly money, with a £5 note on the outside, a toy guitar and a curtain ring for the wedding ring.

Ugly Sisters (for boys and girls!)

Anything goes for these outfits! Very brightly clashing colours for shirts and blouses. Let them wear bloomers (thermal underwear will do!) and stripy stockings if you have them. Large shoes. Tie hair up with lots of bows all in different colours and very exaggerated hideous make-up.

Indian and Squaw

In summer decorate a boy's chest, back and face with war paint, using suitable face paints. Stick some feathers on to a band to fit your child's head. Put him into suitable trousers or jeans and moccasin shoes or slippers, if possible. Give him a bow and arrow to carry.

A squaw can wear a tunic, fringed if possible, moccasins, a head band and feather, and could paint her face. Two black woollen plaits could be fixed to the head band.

Peter Pan and Wendy

For Wendy a nightdress. She could be hugging a teddy bear, and wearing slippers. Peter Pan in a green tunic (see page 30), or a green, belted shirt as for the Knave of Hearts. Give Peter Pan a large box labelled flying powder.

Other Pairings

Witch and Cat
See pages 35 and 28 for each outfit.

Alice and the White Rabbit
See pages 35 and 28 for each outfit.

Chef and Waitress
See pages 23 and 33 for outfits.

Dick Whittington and His Cat
See pages 27 and 28 for outfits.

Doctor and Nurse
See pages 23 and 32 for outfits.

Wurzel Gummidge and Aunt Sally
See page 24 for Wurzel and Aunt Sally outfits.

Presents

You could give little presents as prizes for winning games, and most people give small going-home presents at the end of the party, as well as a balloon, to each child. Instead of simply handing out presents at the end, it is more fun to wrap each little gift either in tissue paper, or used wrapping paper (iron it if creased). Have a present hunt at the end of the party, having hidden them either around the house, or if the weather is fine, around the garden. This is ideal for younger children whose mothers have stayed with them, and who can help them find the presents. For older children have a bran tub or box, and decorate it with crepe paper, tied around with a big ribbon. Cut out lots of strips of newspaper and put these in the box with the presents.

If you are inviting both sexes to the party, then remember that the presents should be suitable for both boys and girls, or else make separate boy/girl presents, and wrap the girls' presents in pink paper, and the boys' in blue. You can of course put your guests' names on their respective presents. If it is Christmas, then Santa Claus can appear suitably garbed, anonymous, and armed with a sack full of goodies. If you are privileged enough to have an inglenook fireplace, put a pair of kitchen steps inside the fireplace, and at the end of the party 'find' Father Christmas 'coming down the chimney', lightly sprinkled with soot! Younger children are totally captivated by this.

The presents need be only small, although depending on the number of your guests, it is amazing how fast the 10p's add up! Or if you have time, try and make some goodies yourself.

Bought Presents

Either from the local toy shop, in the pocket money section, or from W. H. Smith or Woolworth:

Pencil sharpeners
Little books
Little pencils and notebooks
Sweets – tiny packets of Smarties, fun-size Mars Bars, or perhaps a packet of sugar cigarettes.
Sweet lollipops – if outside and fine weather, suspend them from the branches of a tree for a lollipop tree.
Toys – a cheap farm animal, car etc, to carry through your party theme.

Home-made Presents

Felt Finger Puppets

You can buy felt at a local craft shop. It is probably worth asking if they have any off-cuts, if you do not need the felt for any other purpose. If not, buy a small amount of felt in different colours. We have given you several designs to choose from – rabbit, pirate, owl, little girl, cat – or you can design your own puppet, around your party theme perhaps. The finger puppets can either be sewn or glued. If you choose the latter method, then we suggest a clear adhesive like Bostik.

Cut out your finger shape, approximately $2\frac{1}{2}$ inches long (6 cm) long by $1\frac{1}{2}$ inches (3·5 cm) wide (this is to allow for your glued or sewn seam). Cut another matching piece and either glue or sew together. If you are making an

animal which requires ears, you could insert these between the two halves prior to the gluing or sewing, or you could sew them on afterwards. Cut out contrasting colour eyes, mouth, or animal nose, and glue these in the appropriate place. It always looks more realistic to add a little tiny pupil to the eye and the mouth can be simply made by cutting a triangle and with the long base side at the top, this gives a smile effect. To produce suitable ears, beak, etc, follow the diagrams. For animal whiskers, thread a needle and with the cotton doubled pass the needle at the nose point, just through the snout, and cut to a suitable length and repeat until you have sufficient whiskers, as in the diagram. If you wish to make hair for the little girl, use pieces of wool, or embroidery thread glued at a centre parting, and tie the wool or thread in bunches at ear level, with bits of either very narrow ribbon or contrasting threads. You could easily cut out hat shapes, buttons or collars to put on top if you wish.

Egg Cosies

For an Easter Party make little egg cosies. Make them in the same way, using the same design suggestions, as for felt finger puppets, but sew rather than glue the seams. The two pieces of felt should be 2 inches (5 cm) high and $3\frac{1}{2}$ inches (9 cm) wide. Include a small chocolate Easter egg.

Bean Bags

Use odd remnants of material (don't worry if these are all totally different, do one side one design and the other another). Cut the material into approximately 7 inch (17·5 cm) squares, and machine sew up very firmly, with a double seam to make approximately 6 inch (15 cm) square bags. Leave a small hole at one corner, and then turn the bag inside out, so that your seams are on the inside. Fill with dried peas, or whatever you choose, and sew up the hole very firmly. These should perhaps not be given to younger children, depending on the firmness of your stitching!

Masks

Make a mask-shaped template out of news-paper and cut your masks out of coloured firm paper or card. Then make your two eye holes, and decorate the mask with self-adhesive coloured shapes, which you can buy in packets. If you wish you could put clear adhesive on part of the mask and sprinkle with glitter. Make two small holes on either side, and using your child as a guide to the size, attach either shirring elastic or a single piece of wool or ribbon from each hole, to tie at the back of the head. It is a good idea to place hole reinforcers over the holes first, to strengthen them. (See the mask invitations on page 22).

Peg Dolls

You can still buy the old fashioned springless type of peg at ironmongers. It will depend on your ability as a seamstress as to how elaborate you make these peg dolls, but using a few remnants of material and felt you can make very satisfactory gifts without much expertise. In fact, you can use a clear adhesive glue like Bostik, instead of sewing, to keep the making of the doll very simple.

First of all make the doll's face. As these pegs are unvarnished you may find biro the easiest medium to work with, as it will not 'splodge'. If you have any model enthusiasts in the family 'borrow' a little enamel paint and paint the doll's face. If you have time and energy, perhaps paint the feet of the doll black, otherwise just leave them plain. Then twist a piece of pipe-cleaner around the doll's neck to form the two arms. Then make the dress, add sleeves if you can, then finish off with pink felt for her hands. If you are making a girl doll, then you could put a little petticoat underneath the main piece of material for the outer garment. Don't forget to trim her with the odd piece of lace, which gives a more professional finish. To make your doll's hair, you could glue either embroidery thread or wool. You may need to catch it back in bunches, either with a couple of little stitches or a thin ribbon bow, to prevent the hair sticking out too much.

Home-made Sweets

These sweets are really quite easy to make and are popular presents. Wrap three or four sweets together in cellophane and tie with a pretty ribbon.

Peppermint Creams

See photograph on page 76.

10 oz (275 g) icing sugar, sieved
1 egg white, stiffly beaten
A few drops of peppermint essence
Green food colouring
Cellophane or cling film
Very narrow satin/nylon ribbon or wrapping ribbon

Add the sieved icing sugar to the whisked egg white, and mix with a wooden spoon (if not stiff enough add a little more icing sugar). Stir in the peppermint essence, and green food colouring. Roll out the peppermint mixture on to a board sprinkled with icing sugar, and cut out shapes (diamonds, stars etc) with a knife or the smallest sized pastry cutter, or suitably sized lid.

Leave the peppermints in a cool place until they are set hard (this may take several hours). Then cut pieces of cellophane or cling film into 6 inch (15 cm) squares, and wrap the peppermints up, gathering up the ends and securing them with pretty, narrow ribbon.

Fudge

1 lb (450 g) sugar
5 oz (150 g) butter
¼ pint (150 ml) milk
Cellophane or cling film
Narrow ribbon (as for Peppermint Creams)

Grease a tin about 8 inches (20 cm) square. Put all the ingredients into a saucepan over a gentle heat and stir until the sugar is dissolved. Bring to the boil, stirring all the time, and boil until a small spoonful of the mixture dropped into a cup of cold water forms a small ball. Take off the heat and beat for a couple of moments until the mixture has cooled slightly. Pour into the tin and cut into squares when cold. Wrap as in Peppermint Cream recipe.

Chocolate Fudge

Make as above, adding 2 tablespoons cocoa, and make sure the cocoa is completely dissolved before the mixture comes to the boil.

Gingerbread Men

These are rather large for small children to eat as part of a tea, so they make interesting take-home gifts wrapped in cling film. Have some spare ones, in case of breakages, and if you have time pipe your guests' names on them. See page 86 for the recipe.

Toffee Apples

6–8 unblemished eating apples
1 lb (450 g) demerara sugar
2 oz (50 g) butter
¼ pint (150 ml) water
2 tablespoons golden syrup
One wooden stick per apple (or lolly stick)

First of all prepare your apples: wipe them clean, dry them and insert the sticks. In a large heavy bottomed pan, melt the remaining ingredients over a gentle heat (do not stir too much as this may cause the toffee to crystallize). When the sugar has dissolved, boil rapidly for about 5 minutes, until the temperature is about 290° F (143° C) or test the toffee by popping a little into cold water – it should divide into fairly hard threads. Remove the pan from the heat. Tipping it slightly, dip in your apples and coat each one completely. Stand the apples either on a buttered tray or on wax paper. When quite cold, wrap each one in a piece of cellophane or waxed paper, and hold with a ribbon, rubber band or freezer twist tie. You can prepare these toffee apples a couple of days before the party, but keep them somewhere dry.

Peanut and Chocolate Balls

3½ oz (100 g) plain chocolate
1 oz (25 g) butter
2 oz (50 g) peanuts
1 teaspoon vanilla essence

Break up the chocolate, put in a bowl and stand over a pan of hot water. Add the butter and leave until both are melted. Chop the peanuts coarsely and add to the chocolate with the vanilla essence. Form into balls, and leave to firm before wrapping.

Coconut Ice

Makes 64 pieces

1 lb (450 g) sugar
¼ pint (150 ml) milk
5 oz (150 g) desiccated coconut
pink colouring

Grease a tin, 8 × 8 inches (20 × 20 cm) square. Put the sugar and milk into a saucepan and heat gently until the sugar has dissolved. Bring to the boil, stirring continuously, and cook until a spoonful dropped into cold water forms a soft ball. Remove from the heat and stir in the coconut. Pour half the mixture into the tin, add pink colouring to the remaining half and then pour over the first portion. Divide into 1 inch (2.5 cm) squares while the coconut ice is cooling. Don't take out of tin until completely cold.

Party decorations

It is a good idea to show where the party is being held by putting a bunch of balloons on your gate post or front door. If you are intending to have a theme running throughout the party, start it off by drawing a suitable poster, or make a cut-out concertina of dolls or animals, such as elephants joined trunk to tail, to reflect the theme, and attach these to the gate or front door. See the invitation section for ideas.

Balloons

Lots of balloons around the house will give a festive atmosphere without much effort or inconvenience other than a lot of puff from someone! If you are desperate you can buy a balloon pump from stationers. Once you have blown the balloons up you can write each child's name on a balloon or draw faces on them with a felt-tipped pen. Always remember to have some extra balloons in case of accidental bursts! Tie a piece of string, wool or ribbon to each balloon, and, mixing the colours and shapes, group them into however many bunches you require to decorate the room. Tie a slip knot in the bunch of strings so that when the children go home you can easily take the balloon cluster down and free them by simply pulling the right end.

The Party Room

If you are having your party at home, clear the room that you have chosen for the games of all breakable objects to avoid any embarrassing accidents. If you are lucky enough to have a nursery or play room, then hold the party there, and, depending on your time and energy, decorate the room to the best of your ability. If you can carry the party theme through from the invitations into decorations then do so. Use posters or drawings of the chosen theme, sheets of wrapping paper of a suitable design, record sleeves, pictures from magazines, etc. Use sheets of silver foil for a spaceman's party. Blu-tack is ideal to use as an adhesive for these, but obviously it depends on the surface of your wall. If you wish to make your decorations, you could have more strings of concertina figures as you did for the outside of the house, strung on the walls indoors.

Streamers

One easy but effective form of decoration is crepe paper streamers. Keep the paper folded as in its original packet, cut it across into 2 inch (5 cm) strips, then frill the edges by running the back of the scissors down either side. Unwind the strips, join ends with sellotape (you can buy double sided sellotape which is expensive, but extremely strong and durable), twist the strips and fasten around the walls and across the ceiling with Blu-tack. Don't destroy these decorations as they will come in handy for other occasions.

If you are having your party in a hall, then go down there well before the party date, have a look around and see if there is any way in which you can quickly and easily decorate before the party. Often at these places one can only have the hall a little while before your party is due to start, and you may well find that you have no time at all to decorate. However, if you do have time, remember that in a room of large proportions small decorations get rather

lost, and plenty of streamers and balloons and the like are probably the most effective way of decorating.

Party Tea

If you have the space, we suggest that you set tea in another room, simply to avoid over-enthusiastic premature nibblings! If you are planning to use your dining-room table, or any wooden table for the tea party, then cover it first of all with a polythene sheet (cleaner's bags sellotaped together will suffice) and place your cloth on top. Use benches if you have any, as they take up less room than chairs, but try not to overcrowd your guests; each child takes up more room than one would imagine.

The Tea Table

You can buy very attractive matching paper sets, which include table cloths, napkins, mugs, plates in varying sizes, and jelly containers. These are expensive, but labour saving (wash up unstained items at leisure and keep them for picnics, and they will not be quite as extravagant as they might seem at first sight). However, you can make the table look very attractive using your own equipment, so long as you have enough. Instead of napkins, you could economize by using coloured kitchen roll, folded into individual squares for each child. A cheerful gingham tablecloth will not need further decoration, but a plain white cloth could be jollied up with foil strips, cut out and stapled in criss-crosses over the cloth, or cut-out shapes of animals, stars, moons, in foil or coloured card which might fit in to your party theme and again could be stapled to the cloth. If you are not using paper sets then try and make sure that your colours at least blend, even if you haven't sufficient matching equipment. But remember not to use glasses for small children to drink from. If you have time, cut out place names from coloured card – carrying on the theme or simply cut oblongs, fold them in half, write each child's name on one and stand them on their long sides. Use pinking shears to give a fancy edge, if you like.

If you have room on your table, and if you don't mind the prospect of games being played while eating progresses, then decorate your table further by putting plastic animals, if you have an animal theme, or small cars, etc, around the table. Suspend a bunch of balloons or Blu-tack some mobiles over the tea table. The sets of bought plates, etc, often come in packets which do not necessarily match up with the numbers of guests, so if you have any of these left over, it is very easy to thread a piece of cotton through the rim of one of these, knot the thread, and use this as a mobile above the table. You could make foil or coloured card shapes, and similarly suspend these. Remember that it is best to glue the foil to firmer card as it may curl up with the heat in the party room, and lose its effect.

2. PARTY CAKES

However daunting it may be for the mother, the focal point of any child's tea party is the cake! The climax lies in the candle blowing and singing ritual, not in eating the master-piece – so don't be disappointed or offended if most of the cake is left (you can always cut up slices to be taken home in paper napkins, if you've time). Nevertheless, the centrepiece must be on show, and the more interesting or amusing, the more likely it is to be devoured. If your party has a specific theme, try to keep the cake in line with it, or, if your child asks for a specific cake such as a train or a ship, then shape your ideas for the party around it. In our cake section we provide lots of ideas for different cakes which look effective and can be achieved quite simply.

Once you have decided on your cake, then is the time to think of the rest of the party food.

In this chapter we provide detailed recipes for the basic cakes and icings. These are followed by the recipe for each individual cake which tells you which basic cake is required, and we have numbered these basic cakes for extra clarity. Don't worry at all if your cake might look a little crooked, bumpy or otherwise not quite perfect – it all adds to the charm of a home-made cake and the children will love it.

We have both experienced the feeling of horrible inadequacy when our children have demanded what seems like an impossibly exotic cake – 'Make me a hedgehog/a car/a space ship/a house' – but our recipes are genuinely easy to follow and we promise that most effective results can be achieved even by the most unconfident or inexperienced cake-maker.

If you have never made a cake before, then start off with the all-in-one sponge. This is the never-fail cake with a light perfect texture. Use it to make one of the simpler cakes which do not require any shaping; the zoo cake, clock, or football match, for instance. As the texture tends to be rather brittle, we do not recommend it for any of the cakes which need cutting into shape. But it does keep very well so you can make it two or three days in advance.

If you are making a Victoria sponge, you can make it two days before the party and ice it the day before. This gives time for the icing to harden and avoids last-minute panics on the party day itself. Alternatively any cake made with butter icing can be made in advance, iced, and put into the freezer on a cake board. Take it out on the morning of the party. Don't freeze a cake decorated with glacé icing – the colour goes blotchy and the icing tends to melt on defrosting. Smarties do not freeze well and should be added as decoration on the day of the party.

We have also included a section on ice cream cakes, which are extremely easy to make, and very popular with children. We have found by experience that it is not a good

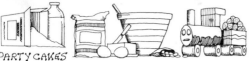
idea to mix ice cream and sponge in the same cake – the sponge gets soggy and the children don't eat it – so, other than the snow princess which requires a sponge base, our ice cream cakes can be assembled from start to finish in a few minutes. For the sake of hygiene, we have made sure that instructions do not involve a lot of refreezing of the ice cream – in most cases the cake can be assembled in one operation and put straight back in the freezer until required.

Cake boards come in many shapes and sizes. However, a large table mat or bread board, covered with foil with the shiny side up, can be a cheap but effective alternative.

We know that time is the vital factor. Due to unforeseen circumstances (the typical experience of any mum!) one of us had ten minutes to assemble the crinoline lady doll cake one day – but it worked and looked lovely.

Metric conversions are approximate, so stick to either metric or imperial in any one recipe. Finally, don't forget the matches – and, why not try the candles that relight themselves.

Basic cakes and cake ideas

Basic Swiss Roll

Oven Temperature: 425°F, 220°C, Gas Mark 7

3 large eggs
3 oz (75 g) caster sugar
3 oz (75 g) self-raising flour, sieved
4 level tablespoons warmed jam, or softened butter icing (see page 49)

Preheat the oven and grease and line a swiss roll tin of 8 × 12 inches (20 ×30 cm). Whisk the eggs (at room temperature) with the sugar, until the mixture is light and fluffy. (There should be a trail when the whisk is taken out of the mixture.) Using a metal spoon, fold in the flour.

Turn this mixture into the tin, and level with a palette knife. Bake in the hot oven for 7–10 minutes, until the sponge begins to shrink from the edge of the tin, and is firm to the touch.

Turn the cake out on to a sheet of greaseproof paper which has been dredged with caster sugar. Trim off the edges of the cake, and roll up tightly with the paper inside. When it is cool, unroll the cake gently, remove the paper, and spread the cake with either jam or the softened butter icing, and then reroll it. If you are using jam, warm it to make it easier to spread, but do not make it too hot, or it will soak into the cake.

Basic Victoria Sponge Cake

Oven Temperature: 350°F, 180°C, Gas Mark 4

6 oz (175 g) soft butter or margarine
3 large eggs
6 oz (175 g) caster sugar
Pinch of salt
6 oz (175 g) self-raising flour, sieved
1 tablespoon milk or water, if necessary

Preheat the oven to the required temperature. Grease your chosen tin or bowl and line the base with greased greaseproof paper, with silicone paper or butter paper cut to fit. It is very important to have your fat and eggs at room temperature, and to warm your mixing bowl.

Cream the fat, sugar and salt until the ingredients are thoroughly combined and the texture is like whipped cream. Beat the eggs in a separate bowl and add them to the creamed mixture a little at a time, beating well after each addition, until the mixture returns to its fluffy state. Sift the flour into the bowl from a height, thereby allowing the flour to take in air. Carefully fold in the flour with a metal spoon. Add the milk or water if the mixture does not fall easily from the spoon.

Turn the mixture into the prepared tin or bowl and bake for the appropriate time (see below). To test if the cake is cooked, press it and if it springs back into shape, it is ready. (Another sign of the cake being thoroughly cooked is when it starts to shrink away from the sides of the cake tin or bowl.) Take out of the oven and after a minute run a palette knife around the edge of the container and turn the cake on to a wire tray. Peel off the greaseproof paper and allow to cool.

Flavour and Colouring Suggestions

Vanilla: $\frac{1}{2}$ teaspoon vanilla essence – add to the fat and sugar
Chocolate: 1 tablespoon cocoa powder – add to the flour, sieved
Orange: 1 teaspoon grated rind and juice from $\frac{1}{2}$ orange – add to fat and sugar
Lemon: 1 teaspoon grated rind and juice from $\frac{1}{2}$ lemon – add to fat and sugar
Marble: A few drops of pink colouring, and 1 dessertspoon chocolate powder. This makes a very pretty three colour cake. Divide the prepared sponge mixture equally between three bowls, then colour one pink, one chocolate, and leave the last one plain. Take 1 tablespoon from each bowl, and drop it into the prepared baking tin or bowl. Continue until the mixture is used up. Slightly hollow the centre of the cake and give *one* swirl with a metal spoon. Place in the centre of the oven, and bake according to the specific instructions for the shape of the tin or bowl used.

Basic Cakes 1–8

1. Two round sandwich cakes, baked in 8 inch (20 cm) sandwich tins. 20–25 minutes.
2. One square cake, baked in 8 inch (20 cm) square cake tin. 45 minutes.
3. One round cake, baked in 8 inch (20 cm) sandwich tin. 30–35 minutes.
4. One loaf shaped cake, baked in loaf tin, top approximately 9 × 5 × 3 inches (22·5 × 12·5 × 7·5 cm). 50–55 minutes.
5. Two basin shaped cakes, baked in $\frac{1}{2}$ pint (300 ml) and $1\frac{1}{2}$ pint (900 ml) pudding

basins, each two-thirds full. (Use white china pudding basins, as pyrex are too flat bottomed.) Cooking time for large basin, 1 hour; for small basin, 30–35 minutes.

6. One large 2 pint (1·1 litre) pudding basin. (Again use white china basin rather than pyrex.) 1 hour 15 minutes.

7. Rectangular cake, baked in swiss roll tin 8 × 12 inches (20 × 30 cm). 30–35 minutes.

8. One ring mould cake, baked in 9 inch (22·5 cm) ring mould tin. 40 minutes.

Basic All-in-one Sponge Cake

Oven Temperature: 325°F, 170°C, Gas Mark 3

8 oz (225 g) self-raising flour
1¾ level teaspoons baking powder
8 oz (225 g) soft margarine
8 oz (225 g) caster sugar
4 large eggs

Preheat the oven, grease the baking tin(s), and line with silicone or greaseproof paper.

Sift the flour and baking powder into a bowl, shaking the sieve from quite high above the bowl, so that the flour takes in air. Add all the other ingredients, and whisk well (with an electric hand beater if you have one) for about a minute until well mixed. The mixture should be firm but not stiff – add 1 or 2 tablespoons of warm water if necessary until it is the right dropping consistency. Spoon it into the prepared tin(s), smooth the surface and cook in the centre of the oven for the required time (see below), until well risen and golden.

Gently press the cake with a finger and if it springs back into shape, it is cooked. Remove from the oven, allow to cool in the tin for a couple of minutes, run a palette knife around the sides of the tin then turn out on to a cake rack. Remove the paper very carefully, and leave until cool.

Flavour and Colouring Suggestions

Vanilla: ½ teaspoon vanilla essence – add to the margarine and sugar
Chocolate: 1 tablespoon cocoa powder – add to the flour, sieved
Orange: 1 teaspoon grated rind and juice from ½ orange – add to margarine and sugar
Lemon: 1 teaspoon grated rind and juice from ½ lemon – add to margarine and sugar

Basic Cakes 9–10

9. Two round sandwich cakes, baked in 8 inch (20 cm) sandwich tins. 20–25 minutes.
10. One rectangular cake, baked in a swiss roll tin 8 × 12 inches (20 × 30 cm). 45–50 minutes.

Butter Icing

4 oz (110 g) butter, at room temperature
10 oz (275 g) icing sugar, sieved
1 tablespoon liquid (fruit juice, water or
  milk)

Cream the butter with the appropriate flavouring and gradually beat in the icing sugar, and liquid if required. Beat the mixture until the consistency is smooth and creamy.

Flavourings

Vanilla: ½ teaspoon vanilla essence
Chocolate: 2 level tablespoons sieved cocoa, made into a paste with a little water
Lemon: 1 teaspoon lemon juice, with finely grated rind
Orange: 1 dessertspoon orange juice, with a little finely grated rind
Peppermint: A few drops of oil of peppermint, or peppermint essence with a couple of drops of green food colouring.

Colourings

You can buy food colourings – mix a few drops of whichever colour you wish with the basic icing. For blue icing you may prefer to use glacé or the 'white' butter icing recipe as the yellow of basic butter icing makes the colour rather green.

Apricot Glaze

3 tablespoons apricot jam, sieved
1 tablespoon lemon juice

If you are using glacé icing, you will need to cover the cake with a layer of apricot glaze first to prevent crumbs getting into the icing. Heat the jam with the lemon juice, and push through a plastic sieve into a basin with a wooden spoon. Use this mixture while still warm, but not too hot.

Pure White Butter Icing

4 oz (110 g) softened butter (unsalted, as
  this is the palest in colour)
10 oz (275 g) icing sugar, sieved
2 tablespoons cold milk

Beat the butter until very soft. Continue to beat while gradually adding the sifted icing sugar, alternately with the milk, until all the icing sugar and milk is used up. Continue beating until soft and white. This will make sufficient icing to fill the centre and cover the outside of an 8 inch (20 cm) sandwich cake.

Glacé Icing

8 oz (225 g) icing sugar, sieved
2–3 tablespoons hot water
Flavouring of choice (as in the butter icing
  recipe)
Colouring of choice – use a few drops

Gradually mix the sieved icing sugar with the hot water, beating well until a smooth coating consistency is achieved. Add the hot water very cautiously as it is easy to make the icing too runny. When ready to use it should still seem to be a little stiff – this is the correct consistency. Add the flavouring and colouring as required.

Dougal Cake

1 bought or home-made chocolate swiss roll
(page 46)
Chocolate butter icing (page 49)
1 Wagon Wheel
A few Smarties, to form eyes and nose
Candles and holders

If you can pipe the icing, use the number 8 vegetable nozzle (a large zig-zag nozzle) to pipe from Dougal's centre back downwards on either side to form his shaggy hair. Use the Wagon Wheel and Smarties (stick with a dab of icing) to make his face.

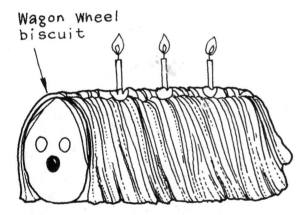

Wagon Wheel biscuit

If you can't pipe then don't panic, but cover the cake with the butter icing, and smooth it with a palette knife. Then draw a line down the centre back, and from that use a fork to draw 'hair' lines down the sides of Dougal. Position candles along his back.

Teddy Bear Cake

2 basin shaped cakes (basic cake 5)
Chocolate butter icing (page 49: save an
egg-cupful)
2 Yoyos
2 Smarties for his eyes
1 Malteser for his nose
4 miniature chocolate covered swiss rolls
Cocktail sticks
2 Munchmallows
Candles and holders

Trim the base of the smaller cake to make the head a better shape. Put the large cake round side up on to a board, fasten the smaller one to it (also round side up) with a little butter icing, and cover both cakes with the rest of the icing. Add one extra

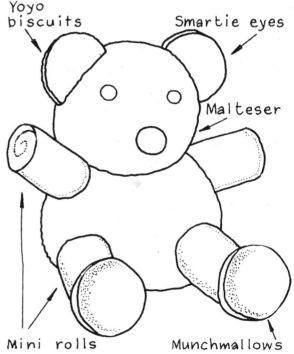

Yoyo biscuits

Smartie eyes

Malteser

Mini rolls

Munchmallows

dollop of icing on one side of the bear's head, where his nose is going to be. Roughen the surface of the cake with a fork. For the bear's ears, cut two slits at the top of the bear's head with a sharp knife, and remove two very small slivers of cake. Put the Yoyos in the spaces provided and place the Smarties and Malteser in position. To make his arms and legs stick a cocktail stick halfway into the four swiss rolls and push the other half of the stick into the cake so that the arms stick out on either side of the bear, and the legs stick out in front, along the board. Use a dab of icing and fasten the two Munchmallows as the bear's feet to the end of his legs. Position candles on top of his head.

Hedgehog Cake

2 ×8 inch (20 cm) round chocolate sandwich cakes (basic cake 1)
Chocolate butter icing, made with 6 oz (175 g) butter, 12 oz (350 g) icing sugar and 3 level tablespoons cocoa (page 49)
1 packet of Matchmakers
2 large packets of chocolate buttons
1 Malteser
2 silver balls
Candles and holders

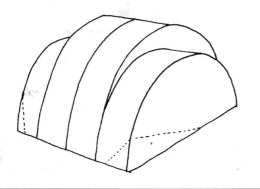

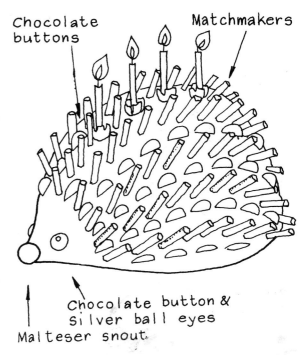

Chocolate buttons

Matchmakers

Chocolate button & silver ball eyes

Malteser snout

Put the two cakes on top of each other and cut straight across them, making slightly unequal portions. Then sandwich the four portions together with some of the butter icing, as shown in the diagram. Shape his face by cutting off a sliver of cake at one end on either side. Form the pointed nose with icing and fill in the gaps between the cakes with extra icing. Cover the cake with the remaining icing, and roughen it a little with a fork. Break the Matchmakers in half and stick these and the chocolate buttons into the icing as his prickles. Stick the two silver balls with a little icing on to his chocolate button eyes. The Malteser becomes his snout. Put candles on his back as extra spines.

Mouse Cake

*2 × 8 inch (20 cm) round orange or
    chocolate flavoured sandwich cakes
    (basic cake 1)*
*Orange or chocolate butter icing, made
    with 6 oz (175 g) butter, 12 oz (350 g)
    icing sugar and 2 dessertspoons orange
    juice and rind, or 3 tablespoons cocoa
    (page 49)*
2 Smarties or chocolate buttons (for eyes)
2 silver balls (for pupils)
1 Malteser (for nose)
*Orange flavoured Matchmakers (about 6 for
    whiskers)*
Thin liquorice (for tail)
2 more chocolate buttons (for ears)
Candles and holders

Assemble the Mouse cake as for the
Hedgehog cake (page 51).

Wise Owl Cake

*2 chocolate basin shaped cakes (basic cake
    5)*
*Chocolate butter icing (page 49: reserve an
    egg-cupful)*
5 chocolate flakes
2 yellow Smarties and 2 silver balls
*1 skinned almond or shelled brazil nut for a
    beak*
Candles and holders

Trim the edges of the smaller cake to make
a rounder shape for the owl's head. Place
the larger cake on a board with the round
end at the top. Sandwich the flat wide end
of the smaller cake to this, using a little of
the icing. Cover the owl with the remaining
icing. Break three of the flakes into slivers

and sprinkle them on to the butter icing,
leaving two circles side by side without
flakes for his eyes. Cut two 1-inch (2·5 cm)
pieces from a flake and press the two
pieces on either side of his head for his ear
feathers. Use a tiny dab of icing to stick the
silver balls to his Smartie eyes, and position
his beak. Cut the rest of the flake in half
and position the pieces as the owl's feet.
Cut the remaining flake in half and press
the pieces into his sides as wings. Put the
candles in their holders around the owl's
ear feathers.

Brazil
nut or
almond
beak→

Cat Cake

*2 × 8 inch (20 cm) round chocolate
  sandwich cakes (basic cake 1)
Chocolate butter icing (page 49)
3 Smarties (2 green for eyes, and 1 orange
  for the nose)
6 thin strips of liquorice or a liquorice
  wheel (or Matchmakers)
1 satin bow
Candles and holders*

Sandwich the cakes together with butter
icing and assemble the cat's ears as in the
drawing.

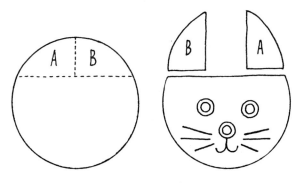

Cover the cat's head and ears all over
with the chocolate butter icing, and
roughen it up with a palette knife to
simulate fur. 'Round' the cat's head between
his ears with extra icing. Place the two eyes
and nose on the cake. Cut the liquorice
wheel into thin strips and surround the eyes
and nose with an outline of liquorice Use six
thin strips of liquorice to make the cat's
whiskers. Shape the nose and mouth as in
the drawing. Sit a satin bow at his chin and
put the candles in his ears.

Butterfly Cake

*8 inch (20 cm) round orange flavoured cake
  (basic cake 3)
Orange butter icing (page 49)
2 packets orange and lemon crystallized
  slices or 1 Terry's crystallized orange and
  1 Terry's crystallized lemon
2 Matchmakers
Candles and holders*

Split the cake in half horizontally and
sandwich together with some of the butter
icing. Then cut it in half vertically, straight
down the middle. Place the two halves of
the cake on the board to form the butterfly
shape, as you can see in the drawing.
Cover with the remaining butter icing.
Make the head of the butterfly with a
rounded blob of icing, and stick the
Matchmakers in as antennae. Arrange the
orange and lemon slices alternately over
the top of the cake, to create the design of
the butterfly's wings. If you are using
Terry's crystallized orange and lemon, cut
the slices in half lengthways before
arranging them, otherwise they are too
thick.

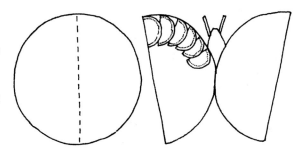

Humpty Dumpty Cake

See photograph facing page 97.

---

1 chocolate loaf shaped cake (basic cake 4)
Butter icing (page 49)
Few drops pink colouring
1 chocolate Easter egg about 5 inches (12·5 cm) high
1 skewer 6–8 inches (15–20 cm) long
Smarties (if not using piping bag)
2 silver balls
3 chocolate finger biscuits
Piece of ribbon 12 inches (30 cm) long
White paper to make Humpty Dumpty's collar and thin ribbon
Candles and holders

Although this is primarily an Easter cake or for birthdays around Easter time, you could make it later in the year, as a bought chocolate Easter egg will keep very well for several months in a cool dry place. It is extremely easy to make, very effective and younger children absolutely love it.

Level off the top of the cake if necessary. Cut in half and sandwich the two halves together with butter icing, as in the drawing. Put two tablespoons of the butter icing into a piping bag (if using one), and leave this in the fridge to harden. Colour the rest of the icing with the pink colouring (quite a deep pink, to represent the bricks). Cover the cake with the icing, and with the point of a knife, mark out the lines of the bricks all over the cake. If you do not wish to do any piping, then the bricks look quite effective as they are, but piping is very simple to do, and does look more striking. It does not matter if it is not quite accurate, in fact, this makes it look more like an old brick wall! Pipe along the lines made by

the knife point through a small nozzle. Do not use all the white icing, save the last little bit for Humpty Dumpty's face.

Make Humpty Dumpty's collar by following the diagram. To prepare Humpty Dumpty take a sharp knife and very gently scrape away some of the chocolate at the blunt end of one half of the egg. Remove just enough to make a hole for the head of the skewer to go through. Fill the egg with Smarties (the weight also helps him to balance). Tie the two halves of the egg together with the collar and the ribbon, making a nice bow in the centre of the collar. Push the skewer into the cake, making sure it tilts backwards and lower the egg gently on to the skewer, sitting it firmly on the cake. Then pipe in eyes, eyebrows, nose and mouth. If you are using Smarties for his face, then place these in

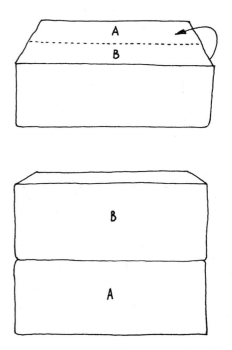

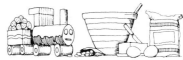

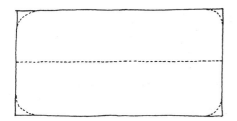

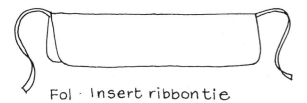

Cut out collar from white paper
Trim corners and fold

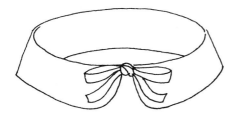

Fol · Insert ribbon tie

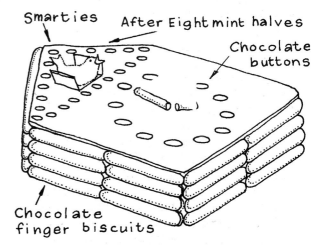

Cuckoo Clock Cake

8 × 12 inch (20 × 30 cm) rectangular
chocolate cake (basic cake 7)
Chocolate butter icing (page 49)
1 packet of chocolate fingers or
Matchmakers
1 packet of chocolate buttons
2 Matchmakers or a chocolate finger cut in
half
1 packet of Smarties
1 bird (the robin off the Christmas cake!)
1 After Eight mint as the cuckoo's door (cut
in 2 halves)
Candles and holders

Cut two corners from one end of the cake
to form the inverted V shape of the roof.
Cover the cake with the butter icing.
Decorate with the chocolate fingers or
Matchmakers and the chocolate buttons
(pipe with numbers if you wish). Place the
Smarties around the edge of the cake and
straight across below doorway. Position
mint halves and bird as in drawing.
Position the candles around the cake.

position with a little butter icing. Place the 2
silver balls in the centre of his eyes.

Finally make his legs by cutting two
chocolate fingers in half, and place the
pieces on the cake so that his knees stick
outwards. Then cut about ½ inch (1·25 cm)
from either end of the remaining chocolate
finger, and place these two pieces for his
feet, sticking them out from the ends of his
legs. When positioning your candles along
the cake, remember not to place them too
near to Humpty in case he melts!

Smarties   After Eight mint halves
Chocolate buttons
Chocolate finger biscuits

Clock Cake

2 × 8 inch (20 cm) round chocolate
sandwich cakes (basic cake 1 or 9)

Either (a)
White butter icing (page 49)
12 chocolate buttons
2 chocolate fingers
Small amount of glacé icing to pipe the
numerals on to the clock face on the
chocolate buttons
Candles and holders

Or (b)
Chocolate butter icing (page 49)
12 varying coloured Smarties
2 chocolate fingers
Candles and holders

Sandwich the cakes together with a third of
the butter icing and cover with the
remainder.

If using ingredients (a), place the
chocolate buttons to represent the hours of
the clock, and the chocolate fingers as the
hands of the clock. Use the glacé icing to
pipe the numerals on to the chocolate
buttons and place the candles around the
edge of the cake.

If you are using ingredients (b), place the
Smarties at the points of the clock, and the
chocolate fingers as the hands. Don't worry
about piping the numerals.

This is a very quick and easy cake.

House Cake

See photograph facing page 65.

8 inch (20 cm) square vanilla cake (basic
cake 2)
Chocolate butter icing (page 49)
1 small bought chocolate covered swiss roll
1 packet chocolate fingers
White glacé icing and piping bag with
small nozzle or 1 packet cigarette sweets
to make the windows and doors
1 packet of Smarties for the garden and
bought sugar icing flowers
Green butter icing
Candles and holders

Cut the cake into three sections, as in the
first diagram. Sandwich it together with
butter icing, and assemble it as in the
second diagram.

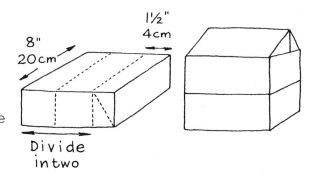

8"
20cm
1½"
4cm
Divide
in two

Cover the whole cake with the remaining
butter icing. Roughen the surface of the roof
with a fork in a downwards direction, to
simulate thatch. Smooth the rest of the
house with a palette knife. Cut the swiss roll
in half and place the halves at either side of
the roof as chimneys. Press the chocolate
fingers into the icing along the top and
around the edge of the roof to form the

ridge, the eaves, and the gables, as in the photograph. If you are using white glacé icing for the windows and doors, make sure it is very stiff, spoon it into the piping bag and pipe two windows and a door on either side of the house, and a window at each end. If you are using cigarette sweets, cut off the pink end and split them in half lengthways with a sharp knife, then put these in position as window and door frames. Use two of the Smarties for door handles. Stick a candle into each chimney and the rest along the top of the roof (on either side of the chocolate fingers).

Make the garden by spooning the green icing on to the board to make a lawn on either side of the door. Continue the icing round the sides of the house and press the Smarties upright around the edge of the lawn to represent flower beds. If you are using sugar flowers then arrange these in little groups around the edge of the lawn or have them growing up the cottage walls.

Merry-go-round Cake

8 inch (20 cm) round orange flavoured cake (basic cake 3)
Orange flavoured butter icing (page 49: save an egg-cupful)
7 stripy paper (not plastic) drinking straws
1 ice cream cone
6 small plastic riderless horses (anything suitable to represent the equipment on a real merry-go-round)
Paper frill (striped)
Candles and holders

Cover the top of the cake with the butter icing. Hold the cone wide side up and fill it with butter icing. Push one upright straw

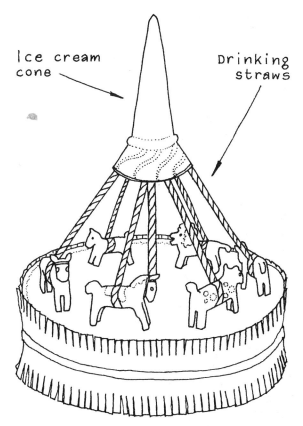

into this. Smooth some icing into every other division inside the lip of the cone and press the remaining straws into it. Turn the cone upside down, and push the centre straw into the centre of the cake. Bend the edges of the outside straws and secure them round the middle of the horses with sticky tape.

Fasten frill. Place the candles around the cake.

Farm Cake

See photograph facing page 65.

*8 × 12 inch (20 × 30 cm) rectangular cake
   (basic cake 10)*
*Half green, half chocolate butter icing
   (page 49)*
Plastic farm animals, tractor, plough, etc
Pottery or plastic farm house, trees, etc
Plastic farm fencing or Matchmakers
Candles and holders

Decide how much of the farm you wish to
be ploughed field, and how much pasture.
Cover the 'ploughed' area with chocolate
icing (mark lines with a fork to simulate
furrows) and place a tractor and plough on
this. Cover the pasture with green icing and
put the sheep or cows on it, together with
the farmhouse, if you have one. Extend the
farmyard round your cake with animals or
farm vehicles surrounding it on the board. If
you wish you could give each child one of
the animals to keep. Position candles.

Sea Cake

Cake as Farm cake
*Blue (sea) butter icing (page 49),
   roughened up as waves (or use blue
   glacé icing and apricot glaze, page 49)*
*Small plastic or wooden sailing ships (tip up
   and down in 'waves')*
*Home-made chocolate fudge for rocks
   (make it uneven)*
Candles and holders (lighthouse by rocks)

Zoo Cake

Cake as Farm cake
Green butter icing or glacé icing (page 49)
Apricot glaze if using glacé icing (page 49)
*Plastic farm fencing or Matchmakers (to
   make enclosures to put animals into)*
*1 packet of Cadbury's chocolate animals,
   wooden or plastic zoo animals (place in
   enclosures, and any extra on board round
   cake)*
*Plastic or wooden trees, etc (to dot around
   as scenery)*
*A few pieces of home-made chocolate
   fudge for rocks (page 40)*
*Small child's mirror or a piece of foil to
   represent a water hole for the sea lion*
Candles and holders
*Place any extra animals on the board
   around the cake*

Village Cake

Cake as Farm cake
Green butter icing for gardens, and chocolate butter icing for road winding across cake (page 49)
Little wooden or plastic houses
Little wooden or plastic church
Plastic dog, pony, people, etc
Candles and holders

Gymkhana Cake

Cake as Farm cake
Green butter icing (page 49)
Matchmakers or plastic farm fencing
Plastic jumps (for main ring)
Plastic ponies and riders strategically positioned
If you have plastic trailers, landrover, etc, put these on the board
Candles and holders

Match Cake

2 × 8 inch (20 cm) square orange or lemon flavoured cakes (basic cake 2) placed together on a board to form an oblong, 16 × 8 inch (40 × 20 cm)
Green butter icing, or apricot glaze and green glacé icing (page 49)
Small quantity of white glacé icing

To make the goals, or goal posts:
Drinking straws or construct-a-straws, cut into correct lengths, sellotaped together, or bent to shape
Malteser or tiny plastic ball

To make a tennis net:
2 cocktail sticks, or 2 chocolate fingers for the posts. Netting from a plastic mesh bag used for nuts or oranges, cut to shape
Candles and holders

Players:
Subbuteo figures and ball if you have them

Place the cakes on the board. Coat the sides of the cakes, and the top with green icing, and smooth with a palette knife. Using a fine nozzle, pipe white lines in the appropriate positions for the game you have chosen, and place the net or goal in position. Place your players on the cake. Place the candles around the edge of the cake.

Crinoline Lady Cake

See photograph facing page 97.

*1 × 2 pint (1·1 litre) basin shaped marble
  cake (basic cake 6)*
Butter icing (page 49)
Pink colouring
*Small plastic doll, approximately 9 inches
  (22·5 cm) high*
*A few inches of lace or other material (to
  make a little bodice for the doll)*
Silver balls
*Bought sugar-icing flowers if you cannot
  pipe*
Pink and/or white candles and holders

This is an exceptionally pretty cake for a
little girl's tea party, and should look
elegant and delicate. It is a simple cake to
produce, and looks very professional.

Prepare the doll before you start
decorating the cake. Remove the legs, and
make a bodice with the material – simple
and strapless. Pin the back or put in a few
stitches to hold it in place.

When the cake is completely cool, make
sure that the bottom is level (if necessary
trim it). Spread three-quarters of the white
icing over the cake, smoothing it with a
palette knife. To create the crinoline effect
of the skirt, mark out the shape of the
paniers (the draped effect of a Victorian
dress) with the rim of a tablespoon (you
should be able to make seven). Make sure
that the markings are even, and at the same
height. Run the handle end of a teaspoon
gently up the lower part of the skirt to
represent the gathers in the material. Take
the doll and press her firmly into the cake.
Mix the remaining icing with a very few

drops of pink colouring so that the colour is
not too bright. If the icing is too soft it will
not pipe well, so put it in the fridge for half
an hour to make it easier to handle. Spoon
this into a piping bag, and practise piping a
few rosettes on to a board. Decorate the
skirt with little rosettes. If you wish you can
put silver balls on these. If you are
using bought decorations place these
carefully around the cake. Place candles
on top of paniers.

Fairy Cake

As for the Crinoline Lady Cake, but add
wings, a wand and a tinsel hair band.

To make the wings use a lace paper doily, rice paper or silver foil. Cut into two triangles. Fasten into the cake at the doll's waist, with a cocktail stick. (Be careful not to position the candles too near the wings or the Fairy may go up in smoke). To make the wand use a cocktail stick, covered with a little foil, and glue or sellotape a little tinsel to the top. To make the hair band, twist a little tinsel around the doll's hair. She makes a very effective Christmas Fairy cake.

Witch Cake

2 chocolate or marble basin shaped cakes (basic cake 5)
Chocolate butter icing (page 49: save an egg-cupful)
1 large chocolate digestive biscuit
1 ice cream cone
A few Smarties
2 silver balls
Several Matchmakers
1 piece of black satin ribbon
2 chocolate fingers for arms
Candles and holders

This cake is ideal for a November 5th or Hallowe'en party.

Place the large cake on your board, flat wide side down. Sandwich the narrow end of the smaller cake to this, using a little of the icing, and trimming the cake, if necessary, to make a good round shape. Cover the witch with the remaining icing. Make the hat from the chocolate biscuit and the ice cream cone, sticking them together with icing. Stick the silver balls on to the Smarties with a tiny dab of icing for her eyes. Place half a Matchmaker to make her

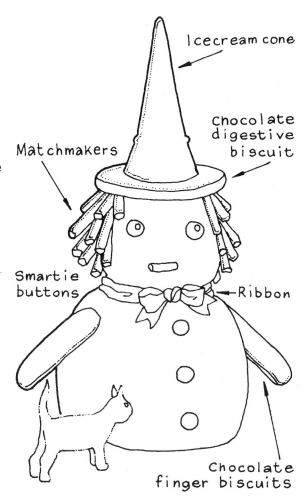

mouth and decorate as in the drawing with the Matchmakers, chocolate fingers, ribbon and Smarties. Position candles on board.

Scarecrow Cake

Adapt the witch. Give him the Snowman's hat (page 62) and a glacé cherry nose. Raise his arms and put a robin on his shoulder.

Space Ship Cake

1 swiss roll, either bought or home made
(page 46)
Chocolate butter icing (page 49: save some
for glueing)
1 Wagon Wheel biscuit
1 cone shaped ice cream cornet
1 packet Smarties
A few silver cake balls
4 After Eight mints
3 small bought chocolate swiss rolls
Plastic spacemen (Lego spacemen are
particularly effective)
Candles and holders

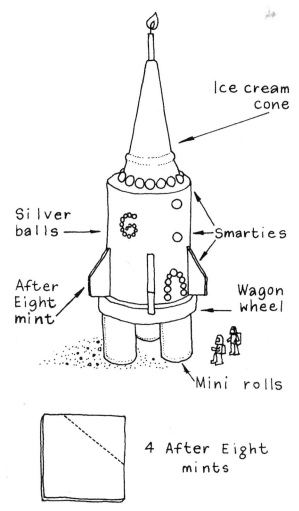

For this cake, first organize the cake board.
A foil-covered board would be best for this
moon-landing cake. If you wish, use some
white glacé or butter icing to simulate the
uneven surface of the moon on the board,
and sprinkle this with some crushed silver
balls. Place the board to one side. If you
are using a home-made roll, it may topple
over if too long, so cut some off.

Stand the swiss roll on end on the Wagon
Wheel using some of the chocolate butter
icing. Cover the entire rocket with
chocolate butter icing and smooth with a
palette knife. Take the ice cream cone and
cut a small hole in its tip, using a very
sharp or fine serrated knife. Fix the wide
end of the cone to the top of the swiss roll
with a little butter icing. Cut a corner of
each mint off diagonally, to make a fin
shape (see diagram), and place the cut side
to the cake securely into the butter icing.
Decorate your rocket. Then put some butter
icing on either end of the three bought
chocolate swiss rolls and stand firmly on
end on the board. Place the assembled
rocket on top of these as in the drawing.

Place one of your candles in its holder
carefully in the hole that you have made in
the ice cream cone (again, you may need
to use a little butter icing in the hole to
secure it). Put the remaining candles at an
angle at the bottom of your swiss roll
rocket, to simulate lift off. Crash land to cut!

This Space Ship cake could be made for
a November 5th party.

Car Cake

1 chocolate loaf shaped cake (basic cake 4)
Chocolate butter icing (page 49: reserve an
egg-cupful)
4 Chocolate Munchmallows
Packet of Smarties
Silver balls
Matchmakers (optional)
Candles and holders

Turn the cake upside down, and cut
segments from either end of the cake as
in the diagram, so that the cake
looks like a car. Cover the car with the
chocolate butter icing and smooth with a
palette knife. Cut two axles about 1 inch
(2·5 cm) wide from the cut-off segments,
and put these on the cake board. Place the
cake on top of the axles. Then 'glue' with
icing the four Munchmallow wheels into
position on the axles and a Smartie as a
hubcap on each.

Decorate the car with the Smarties, silver
balls and Matchmakers, if you are using
them. Place the candles on top of the cake,
and position two as exhaust pipes.

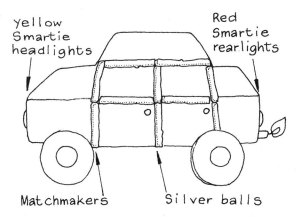

Yellow Smartie headlights

Red Smartie rearlights

Matchmakers

Silver balls

Tank Cake

8 inch (20 cm) square chocolate cake (basic
cake 2)
Chocolate butter icing (page 49)
1 Munchmallow
2 long strips of liquorice
Packet of Rolos
Packet of Smarties
1 Twix
Candles and holders

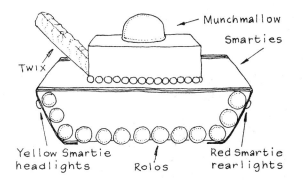

Munchmallow

Smarties

Twix

Yellow Smartie headlights

Rolos

Red Smartie rearlights

Take a 2 inch (5 cm) strip from the side of
your cake. If it has risen up and this would
make the cake lopsided then cut 1 inch (2·5
cm) from either side. Cut the front and the
back of the tank to get the shape. Cover
with the butter icing. Place a piece of the
offcut 2 × 5 inches (5 × 12·5 cm) in the
centre on top of tank and cover with icing.

Place the Munchmallow as the tank's
hatch, your liquorice strips to simulate
caterpillar tracks, and the Rolos to
represent the wheels and have the ones at
either end slightly higher than the rest – cut
your cake here to get the shape. Place the
Smarties as lights, and the Twix as the gun
with the candle secured to 'fire' at the end
of it. Decorate cab with more Smarties.

64 *PARTY CAKES*

Right: Train Cake.
Overleaf: All the fun of the Sack Race.

Train Cake

See photograph opposite.

*2 large bought or home-made chocolate
    swiss rolls (page 46)*
*Chocolate butter icing made with 6 oz
    (175 g) butter, 12 oz (350 g) icing sugar
    and 3 level tablespoons cocoa (page 49)
    (save some for glueing Smarties etc)*
3 long strips of liquorice, or Matchmakers
*5 small bought chocolate covered swiss
    rolls*
1 Munchmallow
1 packet of Smarties
1 packet of Maltesers
8 Rolos
Candles and holders

Lay two flat strips of liquorice or the
Matchmakers on the cake board to
represent the rails. Glue them down with a
dab of butter icing. Cut the other strip in
pieces to lay across the rails as sleepers.
Reserve a small amount for the 'coupling'
between the engine and the coal truck.

Cover one large chocolate swiss roll with
icing, and smooth it with a palette knife.
Place two of the small bought swiss rolls
across the track to represent wheels. Place
the large swiss roll on top of these. The
wheels should be a little in from either end.
Place the third small bought chocolate roll
on the front of the engine as a funnel and
the Munchmallow as the engine's dome.

Cut off about a quarter of your second
swiss roll. Position this, cut side down, to
form the cab and cover with some of the
remaining chocolate butter icing. Place the
Smarties in a circle around the front of the
engine. Using a little icing, place one
Smartie to each side of the swiss roll

wheels (in the centre) to make a hub. Put
bands of Smarties around the engine as
decoration and 4 of the Rolos for buffers. If
you like, decorate with piped chocolate
icing.

Place the last two small bought chocolate
covered rolls on the track behind the
engine. Take the remaining large piece of
swiss roll and cut a hollow out in the centre
to form a container. Cover this with the
remaining chocolate butter icing and place
it on its wheels. Fill the hollow with
Maltesers (to represent coal). Attach the
piece of 'coupling' liquorice from the back
of the engine to the coal container.
Remember to put another Smartie hub on
the wheels of this section and your buffers
in position. Place one or more candles into
the funnel and place the rest along the top
of the engine.

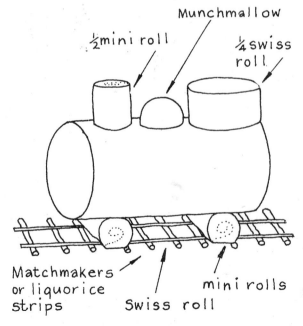

Munchmallow

½ mini roll

¼ swiss roll

Matchmakers
or liquorice
strips

Swiss roll

mini rolls

Tractor Cake

1 large bought or home-made swiss roll
   (page 46)
Chocolate butter icing (page 49)
2 small bought chocolate covered swiss
   rolls
2 Wagon Wheel biscuits
1 packet Smarties
A little green butter or glacé icing
   (optional)
Candles and holders

This cake is very easy to assemble if you
follow the diagram carefully. Use green
icing on the board for the grass and rough
it up with a palette knife. Place two small
swiss rolls on your board. Cut one-third off
the large swiss roll and set the larger piece
on the smaller swiss rolls. (If necessary, cut
the front mini roll in two so that you can see
the 'wheels' on each side.) Cover the large
roll with the butter icing. Position the
Wagon Wheels to form large tractor
wheels.

Cut a small section out of the back end of
the tractor on to which you position the
remaining one-third of swiss roll, cut side
down, to represent the cab. Cover with the
butter icing, and smooth with a palette
knife. Decorate with the smarties. Use a
candle as the exhaust for the tractor.

Tractor Trailer

1 large bought or home-made chocolate
   swiss roll (page 46)
Chocolate butter icing (page 49)
2 small bought chocolate covered swiss
   rolls
Maltesers or Smarties
1 chocolate finger for the coupling

If you are having a particularly large party,
make another swiss roll to use as a trailer
behind the tractor. Cut out the centre top
(see diagram), place the roll on two
chocolate swiss roll wheels, cover with the
butter icing and couple it to the tractor with
the chocolate finger. Pile the Maltesers or
Smarties into the trailer.

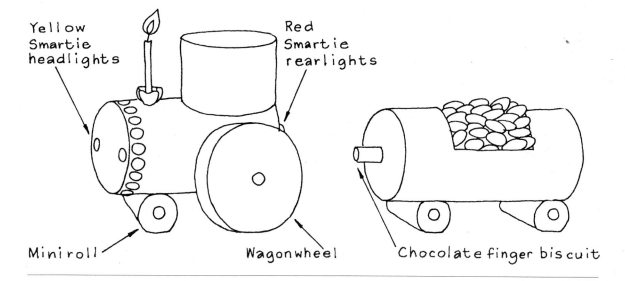

Yellow Smartie headlights

Red Smartie rearlights

Mini roll

Wagon wheel

Chocolate finger biscuit

Castle Cake

8 inch (20 cm) square chocolate cake (basic cake 2)
Chocolate butter icing (page 49: reserve 1 teaspoonful)
4 small bought chocolate swiss rolls (or 8 and put the extra four in the centre of the castle as the keep with arrow slits)
Matchmakers
2 packets of chocolate buttons
1 Penguin biscuit and 2 chocolate fingers
2 strands of liquorice
A little blue icing for a moat (optional)
Plastic knights in armour or plastic guardsmen
1 straw and label with Castle — (your child's name) written on it
Candles and holders

Cut the cake in half horizontally and sandwich the two halves together with butter icing. Trim the corners to allow room for the turrets, and cover with the rest of the icing, smoothing with a palette knife. Place the swiss roll turrets at the cut corners. Arrange the Matchmakers to simulate a stone wall. Using some icing fix matchmaker arrow slits. Place the buttons as battlements and the chocolate fingers as gateposts, the Penguin biscuit and liquorice strands, fixed with icing, as the drawbridge.

If you are using the moat icing, surround the cake with this. Place your plastic knights around the castle, the candles in the turrets and the flag pole in the centre of the cake.

Noah's Ark Cake

See photograph facing page 65.

8 inch (20 cm) round chocolate cake (basic cake 3)
Chocolate butter icing (page 49), reserve an egg-cupful)
1 packet chocolate finger biscuits
1 packet Matchmakers
1 packet Smarties
4 Penguins or similar biscuits
1 packet of Cadbury's Chocolate animals (or plastic animals) and a small plastic man to represent Noah
Candles and holders
Small amount of blue glacé or butter icing for sea (optional)

Cut the cake in half (into half-moon shapes) and sandwich the two halves together with some of the butter icing. Then slice off a *very narrow* sliver from the bottom of the semi-circular slice so that the ark rests on a firm base. Cover the cake with the rest of the butter icing. Run a palette knife along the sides to create a plank effect, or edge the sides with chocolate fingers. Make

straw

CASTLE DANIEL

Mini roll

Chocolate buttons

Matchmakers

Penguin biscuit
Liquorice strands
2 Chocolate finger biscuits

portholes with Smarties, and place more Smarties upright at intervals along the edge of the deck and stick chocolate fingers or Matchmakers (using a little butter icing) along the top to make a deck rail.

Press in four chocolate fingers upright on the deck and stick (again with the butter icing) one of the large biscuits on top to form the roof. Make a ramp with the Penguin biscuits at the end of the Ark. Position the animals going up the ramp and around the deck etc. Place your candles as lights at intervals along the deck rail. Spread the blue icing on the board to represent the sea, and make waves with a fork.

Galleon or Pirate Ship

See photograph on page 44.

8 inch (20 cm) round chocolate cake (basic cake 3)
Chocolate butter icing (page 49)
1 packet of Matchmakers
1 packet Smarties
Rice paper
3 knitting needles
Very fine liquorice strands for rigging
Candles and holders
Optional Extras:
Small quantity of blue icing for the sea
Small pennant with skull and crossbones
Small box with Smarties or gold chocolate coins to represent treasure chest
Maltesers, as cannon balls

Make and assemble as for the Noah's Ark cake to the end of the first paragraph.

To form the sails, cut 3 rectangles of rice paper 8 × 4 inches (20 × 10 cm) and one smaller rectangle 5 × 3 inches (2·5 × 7·5

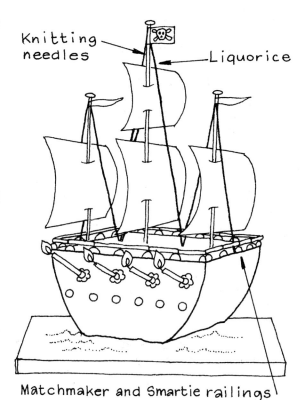

Matchmaker and Smartie railings

cm), then follow the diagram to assemble the sails and masts. If you have time cut out some small pennants to tape or glue to the tops of the masts. If you are making a pirate ship make a skull and crossbones pennant. Sellotape the liquorice carefully across the needles to give the effect of rigging.

Place the treasure chest (if you are using one) on the deck or arrange the Maltesers in neat piles on the deck. If you are making a pirate ship firmly press the end of one chocolate finger flat side upwards on to the deck, so that it makes a plank, and if you have a suitable plastic sailor let him be 'walking' it! Use the candles as cannons.

Cross Road Cake

2 × 8 inch (20 cm) round chocolate
sandwich cakes (basic cake 1)
Chocolate butter icing (page 49: reserve an
egg-cupful)
2 packets of Smarties (reserve 4 red, 4
green and 4 orange)
4 chocolate fingers
White peppermint Tic-Tacs
Model cars, lorries, motor cycles, etc
Candles and holders

Cut the centre out of each of the cakes with a 3½ inch (8·5 cm) cutter – or cut around the rim of a similar sized cup with a sharp knife (use the small cake circles for a tiny extra birthday cake). Place the cake on a largeish board. Cut a sliver off both cakes about 2 inches (5 cm) long on the outer edge. Join the two circles at this point so that you have a figure-of-eight. Cover the cake with the icing and smooth with a palette knife. Use the Smarties, Tic-Tacs and the model cars to decorate the cake as shown in the drawing. Make the traffic lights using the icing to fix on the Smarties to the flat side of the chocolate fingers. Place your candles around the cake as street lights, or on a 'traffic island'.

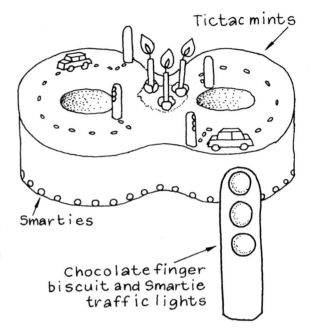

Tictac mints

Smarties

Chocolate finger
biscuit and Smartie
traffic lights

Race Track Cake

The Cross Road cake could be adapted to make either a motorbike or car race track. Have the start at one side of the centre of the figure-of-eight and the end opposite so that there is a continuous track. You could have a green Smartie on a chocolate finger to start the race and a red one to end it, or you could use Scalectrix flags or similar.

Railway Cake

The Cross Road cake can be made into a railway track, using Matchmakers as rails and sleepers with a signal at either end. Place a plastic train and carriages on the track.

Wild West Cake

8 inch (20 cm) square chocolate cake (basic cake 2)
Chocolate butter icing (page 49)
4 small bought chocolate covered swiss rolls
2 packets chocolate fingers
2 Penguin biscuits
1 drinking straw and label, with Fort — (your child's name) written on it
Plastic cowboys or soldiers and Indians
Candles and holders

Cut the cake in half horizontally. Sandwich the two halves together with butter icing, and cover with the rest of the icing.

Place the swiss rolls and chocolate fingers as shown in the drawing. On the fourth side leave a gap in the centre and put the Penguin biscuits as two open gates. Put the drinking straw and label in the centre of the fort as the flag pole, position the cowboys on top of the cake and the Indians around the board attacking.

Position candles on the swiss rolls.

UFO Cake (for failures!)

2 round chocolate cakes (basic cake 3) or whichever cake you have made
Chocolate butter icing (page 49)
4 chocolate flakes, cut in half
8 Smarties
Candles and holders

Dairy milk flakes

Smarties

Chocolate finger biscuits

FORT EDWARD

straw

Mini rolls

Penguin biscuits

If you find that your cake is a complete failure, then just turn it into this unidentified flying object! Sandwich the two cakes together with some chocolate icing and cover with the rest. Roughen it into peaks. Place the chocolate flakes at any old angle, and, using a little of the butter icing, stick a Smartie at the end of each flake to represent lights. Position the candles at random.

Easter Nest Cake

1 chocolate or orange ring mould cake
  (basic cake 8)
Chocolate butter icing (page 49)
4 chocolate flakes
A large quantity of small Easter eggs to fill
  the centre of the ring mould
1 or more Easter chicks (optional)

Cover the nest with the butter icing. Cut
the milk flakes in half widthways with a
sharp knife, and then cut the pieces in half
lengthways to simulate twigs. It doesn't
matter if some of the bits crumble. Arrange
the best bits around the top of the nest, to
make an overlapping circle and then
sprinkle all the remaining bits over the top
– the effect should not be too tidy. Arrange
the eggs and the Easter chicks in the nest.

Snowman Cake

2 marble or vanilla flavoured basin shaped
  cakes (basic cake 5)
White butter icing (page 49: reserve an
  egg-cupful)
1 large chocolate digestive biscuit
1 Munchmallow
5 chocolate buttons for 2 eyes, 3 buttons
1 red Smartie as a red nose
1 Matchmaker or cut-down liquorice pipe
1 piece of satin ribbon as a neck tie or
  scarf (to camouflage the join between the
  head and body of the snowman)
2 chocolate fingers as arms (optional)

Place the large cake, wide flat side down
on the board. Sandwich the narrow end of
the smaller cake to it with a little of the
icing. Trim the smaller cake, if necessary,

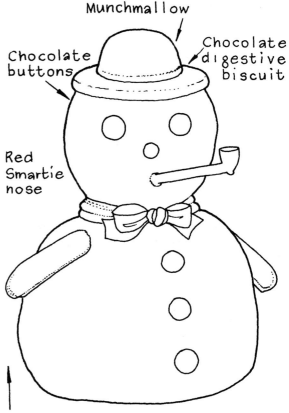

Munchmallow
Chocolate buttons
Chocolate digestive biscuit
Red Smartie nose

Chocolate finger biscuits

to make it a good round shape. Cover the
snowman with the remaining icing. Using a
dab of icing make the chocolate digestive
biscuit and the Munchmallow into his hat.
Place the Smartie, chocolate buttons, the
Matchmaker cigar or the cut-down
liquorice pipe, the scarf, and the fingers
into position.

Snow Scene Cake

*8 inch (20 cm) round chocolate or orange
  cake (basic cake 3)*
White butter icing (page 49)
Crushed silver balls
*Seasonal decorations, such as Father
  Christmas, angels, etc*

Children often do not like the traditional
Christmas fruit cake, so this simple sponge
cake is specifically for them. Cut the cake
in half horizontally, and sandwich the two
halves together with some of the butter
icing. Place the cake on the board, cover
with the rest of the icing and roughen up
the surface into peaks with a fork. Cover
with crushed silver balls and decorations.

Alternatively, sandwich the cake with a
small quantity of butter icing (chocolate or
orange, to match the cake), and cover with
white glacé icing (see page 49).

Christmas Log

*1 bought or home-made chocolate swiss roll
  (page 46)*
Chocolate butter icing (page 49)
2 chocolate flakes
Seasonal decorations (holly, robin, etc)

Place the cake on your board. Cut a
diagonal piece off one end of the cake, and
stick the cut edge with a little icing to the
side of the log to represent a side branch.
Cover the cake with the chocolate icing.
Cut the milk flakes lengthways with a sharp
knife (it doesn't matter if they crumble), and
arrange the bits along the cake to simulate
bark. Arrange the robins and the holly on
top of the cake.

Igloo Cake

1 marble basin shaped cake (basic cake 6)
White butter icing (page 49)
1 packet Matchmakers (optional)
1 small bought chocolate covered swiss roll
Candles and holders

This is the only cake that we recommend
you make in a Pyrex bowl, to get the right
shape.

Cover the cake with white butter icing,
reserving a little, and smooth with a palette
knife. Mark out the lines of the snow blocks
with the point of a knife, or use
Matchmakers. Use half the swiss roll as a
chimney, half as the tunnel doorway. Cover
them both with the remaining icing. Put one
candle on the chimney and the others
around the top of the igloo.

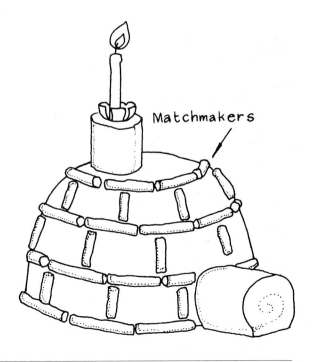

Matchmakers

Numeral Cakes

Special tins can be purchased. Numbers 1 to 9 can be bought at Harrods, Knightsbridge, London SW1, at William Page & Co., 87 Shaftesbury Avenue, London W1, or Divertimenti, Marylebone Lane, London. Many tins can be hired from specialist shops. However, some numbers are easily formed using conventional cake tins. Numbers 1, 3, 7, 8 and 10 can be undertaken as follows.

Number 1

Use a loaf shaped cake (basic cake 4) and if you wish, cut a triangular wedge from the top part of the cake, approximately 2 inches (5 cm) long, to make an angle at the top of your number 1. Cover with butter icing (page 49).

Numbers 3 and 8

Use two ring mould cakes (basic cake 8) and simply place them together on a board to form a figure 8. Cut off a small portion from both to make a good shaped 3. Cover both with double quantity butter icing (page 49). If you do not have a ring mould, use two round cakes (basic cake 1) and cut out the centres with a circular pastry cutter to make your shape.

If you are not having very many people to your party, you could make only one ring mould cake or circular cake, cutting it in half (take out the centre if you are using the circular cake) and then 'glue' the 2 halves together to make the number 3. However, the shape does not look as effective as when you allow more than a semi-circle for each half of the number. If you have made the circular cake, make a little butter icing and sandwich the two leftover circles together to make a little extra cake, either for another day, or to pop in the freezer.

Number 7

Make a rectangular shaped cake (basic cake 7) and cut it as one piece, into your number 7. There will be quite a bit of wastage. Cover with butter icing.

Number 10

Make two cakes – a loaf shaped cake (basic cake 4) and a ring mould cake (basic cake 8). Place them to form the number 10, and cover with a double quantity of butter icing. If you have not got a ring mould, then refer to the instructions for making a number 3.

Initial Cakes

Instead of going through all the letters of the alphabet, here are a few guidelines which, if you refer back to the number cakes, you can adapt to the initial you require.

If you are making a letter which involves straight lines – A, T. Z, H, etc – we suggest that you make it from the rectangular cake (basic cake 7). Place the entire rectangle on the board and cut your cake to shape, keeping it in one piece. Always use a very sharp knife.

For rounded letters, use your ring mould cake (basic cake 8) or cut the centre from a basic cake, numbers 1 or 3, with a pastry cutter. If you haven't the appropriate sized ring moulds, etc, to fit our recipes, adapt what you have, but remember to measure your tins together so that, when assembling your letters, the proportion of one cake balances with that of the other. If you have this problem, cut your cakes to fit – icing hides a multitude of sins!

Ice cream cakes

The ideas we give here are deliberately simple and effortless. You can use all bought ingredients and the time involved in assembling is minimal. We have found that a 'proper' ice cream cake – sponge enclosing a layer of ice cream – is not very popular with children, as they just eat the middle and leave the cake. The most important thing is to have sufficient space either in your fridge or freezer to put your assembled cake in prior to the party. Once removed from the cold atmosphere, don't expect this cake to last for hours! Add candles and holders if appropriate.

There is no reason why you could not simply jolly up a Sunday lunch pudding by using one of these ideas.

Lorry

2 small bought chocolate swiss rolls
1¾ pint (1 litre) family block of Neapolitan
  ice cream
A punnet of strawberries, if in season
4 Jaffa cakes (optional)
Candles and holders

Place the swiss rolls on the board, and cut the ice cream in its carton, into a one-quarter and a three-quarters division. Use the quarter piece to form the cab of a flat fronted lorry, and place the block on the suitably positioned swiss rolls. Put your strawberries on top of the ice cream, as the lorry's load. When you are ready to serve, position your candles along the roof, or at either of the corners of your lorry. If you wish to have larger wheels than the chocolate swiss rolls, then use the Jaffa cakes, and put them in position just prior to serving.

Yellow Teddy Bear's Face

2½ pints (1·5 litres) vanilla ice cream
3 chocolate buttons
1 bow for bow tie (optional)
Matchmakers for whiskers
Candles and holders
(You need an ice cream scoop for this
  cake.)

Pack ice cream into a chilled 8 inch (20 cm) round spring release or loose based tin, and refreeze. Leave some ice cream in the carton, to use with an ice cream scoop later. Before your party, take formed ice cream round out of the freezer, and place on a suitable board. Decorate with ears, made from two scoops of the remaining ice cream. If necessary, replace in the freezer until required. Just before serving decorate the teddy with the chocolate buttons as eyes and nose, and if you wish stick in a few Matchmakers for whiskers, and place his bow tie at his chin, and add candles.

Tractor

2 small bought small chocolate swiss rolls
1¾ pint (1 litre) family block Neapolitan ice
  cream
2 thick slices of Arctic Log
1 chocolate finger
Candles and holders

Place the two chocolate swiss rolls on the board. Cut your ice cream in its carton, into a two-thirds and a one-third division. Cut the one-third in half again. Place the large piece of ice cream on top of the two swiss rolls, and at one end place the two remaining pieces on top of each other to represent the cab. Use the two slices of Arctic Log on either side at the cab end, as large rear tractor wheels. (You need the chocolate roll underneath to have the tractor raised at the back, even though it doesn't show.) Just prior to serving stick the chocolate finger into the engine part of the tractor as the exhaust. Place the candles on the roof of your tractor.

Trailer Cake

If you are having a large party, then add a trailer to the tractor.

3 small bought chocolate covered swiss
  rolls
1¾ pint (1 litre) block of ice cream
  (whichever flavour you wish)
Large punnet of strawberries
1 chocolate finger

Put the swiss rolls on a board. Position the ice cream on top, and pile the strawberries on to the ice cream. Join the trailer to the tractor by sticking the chocolate finger into the back of the tractor and the front of the trailer.

Train

5 small bought chocolate swiss rolls
1 Arctic Log
Bird's Ice Magic
1 choc ice
1 Munchmallow
1¾ pint (1 litre) family block of ice cream
1 Matchmaker, or chocolate finger
Strawberries, if in season
Small amount of chocolate butter icing
  (page 49) and Smarties for decoration
  (optional)
Candles and holders

Place two of the swiss rolls on to a board, and place the Arctic Log on top. Cover the engine with Ice Magic and smooth with a palette knife. Unwrap the choc ice and position it on its side across the top of the log as the engine cab. Then place the dome of the train (the Munchmallow) on the log, and finally the third mini roll, upright, as the funnel of the train. Place the remaining two swiss rolls behind the train and put the family block of ice cream on top as a trailer. Use a chocolate finger or matchmaker as coupling, and put a load of strawberries (if you have them) on the trailer. If you wish, use the chocolate butter icing to fix the Smartie hubs on the swiss rolls and use remaining Smarties to make a face on the front of the engine.

Snow Princess

Oven temperature: 450°F, 230°C, Gas Mark 8

7 inch (17·5 cm) diameter single layer round sponge cake (see below)
5 egg whites
10 oz (275 g) caster sugar
1¾ pint (1 litre) Italiano ice cream (round)
Cheap plastic doll of suitable size, and foil for her bodice (remove her legs)
Sugar flowers
Candles and holders

Follow the Victoria sponge recipe (page 47) but only use *half* quantities. When the cake is completely cold, whisk the egg whites until stiff. Add half the caster sugar, and whisk this mixture again until stiff. Fold in the remaining sugar with a metal spoon. Place the round shaped ice cream on top of your sponge cake, and either spoon the meringue mixture to cover the ice cream, or pipe the meringue, using a large star vegetable nozzle, around the ice cream. Decorate around the top with meringue rosettes, if you wish. It is vital to enclose completely the ice cream within the meringue mixture.

Put the Princess's skirt in the preheated oven and leave for approximately 4 minutes. The meringue should be soft on the inside but a little crisp on the outside. (If you wish you can freeze her at this point. When you wish to serve her you will need to remove her half an hour beforehand, and keep her in the refrigerator.) Then just before serving the Princess, position the top half of your doll (use a piece of foil as her bodice, see page 60) on top of the meringue. Camouflage the join with sugar flowers. If the doll you use has a hollow body with a 'waist' the size of the top of a skewer, you could secure her by putting the skewer in her body and placing the pointed end into the meringue and ice cream.

Clock

1¾ pint (1 litre) ice cream
Chocolate buttons to make a 'frame' for the clock
12 chocolate buttons
2 chocolate fingers
Candles and holders

Pack the ice cream in a chilled 8 inch (20 cm) round spring release or loose based tin, and refreeze. When well set, place the ice cream circle on a board. Just before serving, decorate the very edge of the clock face with chocolate buttons. Place the twelve buttons at each hour, and the chocolate fingers as hands. Place candles around the edge.

3. TEA PARTY FOOD

It is important that the food on the table (apart from the cake of course) should be very small, practically bite size, especially for small children. They will be so excited by the spread of goodies, and so eager to have a taste of everything, that a bite is all they will have in any case, and you don't want to end up with a lot of half-eaten leftovers. For this reason, we have suggested that where a recipe needs paper cases, you use the tiny *petit fours* cases, rather than the ordinary cake sized ones.

There are bound to be leftovers. It is far less nerve-racking for you to know that you have provided too much rather than to risk possible screams of rage because you have run out of a popular item. Leftovers need not be wasted – they can brighten up tea time for the next few days, as all the cakes and biscuit recipes keep well. Leftover sandwiches are excellent toasted or fried, or they can be frozen. One economy tip: don't open all the packets of crisps at once, but keep some back until the first lot are eaten; opened packets don't keep and soggy crisps are sad.

Children love crisps, twiglets, and other savoury nibbles and it is a good idea to buy some ready-made food for the party. You can of course also buy chocolate fingers, iced gems, playbox biscuits, Penguins, etc, but it is very expensive to have nothing but bought food and less satisfying for you, so a mixture of bought and home-made is the best answer. It is not worth providing vast amounts of sandwiches as you will find that with so many other goodies on the table they will only be ignored, but children love savoury food so we have given lots of suggestions for more interesting sandwiches and other savouries.

The first thing is to sit down and plan the menu. Go through the recipe section and make a list of the ones you want to do. At the same time, make a separate list of the ingredients you will need that you don't have in the store cupboard. This will only take five minutes, and saves a lot of time later. All the recipes are extremely easy to make, and require the minimum of cooking and preparation time. Children at parties are not interested in elaborate food, but do want it to look and taste delicious – and it goes without saying that all the following recipes do just that!

Start with one of the jelly recipes for the one to four year olds, and an ice cream recipe for older children, then savouries, followed by sweet things, and finally of course the cake.

Quantities

By now you will know roughly how many guests are coming to the party, and you know how old they are, so you should be able to work out the quantities of food that you will need. Children up to the age of four are usually accompanied by their mothers, and it is surprising how much the mothers can eat!

For this reason we have allowed the same quantities of food for small children's parties as for the older ones.

A rough guide to quantities might be as follows.

For each child:

1 helping of jelly or ice cream (1 packet of jelly makes 8 servings)
¼ packet of family size crisps, potato hoops or other
2 sausages for 2–4 year olds
4 sausages for 5–9 year olds
4 pinwheel sandwiches (the mothers will eat these)
1 bridge roll boat
4 cheese straws
1 Munchmallow
3 shortbread faces
3 coloured meringue drops (some children eat nothing but)
2 little gems
2 chocolate crispies

This is quite a varied menu, but if you want to do less cooking and have a smaller number of different items, you might like to try the following quantities.

For each child:

1 helping of jelly or ice cream
¼ family size packet crisps, etc
3 sausages for 2–4 year olds
4 sausages for 5–9 year olds
4 triple decker sandwiches
1 Penguin, Club, etc
1 Munchmallow
1 peppermint square
1 uncooked chocolate cake

Pre-party Schedule

Having decided on what to eat and how much, the next step is to work out your cooking schedule. We indicate in the recipes whether they can be frozen, or made in advance, and if so how far in advance. Try to make one or two of the recipes each day for a week before the party, rather than leaving everything to the day before and getting in a panic. For instance, make the sandwiches a week early and freeze them (all the recipes freeze well, except those containing egg, which goes leathery). Next make the meringues, flap-jacks, cheese straws, chocolate crispies, etc, and store in a *really airtight tin*. If you don't quite trust your tins, put a layer of greaseproof paper or plastic between the lid and the tin to get a good tight fit. This is vital if you do plan to cook in advance.

Two days before the party make the uncooked chocolate cake, or chocolate truffles, and keep in the fridge. Make the shortbread faces or other shapes, but don't ice them. On this day, you will also have made the cake, but not yet iced it. The day before the party make the jelly or jellies, and keep in fridge. Make, for instance, the cheese scones, ice the shortbread faces (we put them in the airing cupboard overnight to keep them crisp, as you can't stack them into a tin until the icing is really hard). You will also have iced the cake the day before the party.

On the day of the party, take the sandwiches out of the freezer, and slice them while still half frozen. If you haven't frozen your sandwiches, make them now, also make the bridge roll boats, etc. Keep in fridge until required, covered with cling film. In the afternoon, lay the table, arrange your food on plates, cover with cling film and put on table. Check your list to make sure that none of the food is lurking forgotten in your cupboards! Don't forget to put the cake on the table. Arrange the drinks on a side table. Lay cups for mothers (if present) also on a side table, plus milk and sugar. Check that the camera flashlight and film are at the ready for when the candles on the cake are lit and of course, check that the matches are to hand. Check too, that you have several damp cloths for mopping faces and spillages. Finally, just before tea, decorate the jellies or ice creams and put them on the table. Meanwhile, organize the helpers:

1. To take the children to the loo, if required, and wash hands, then to sit them down at table;

2. To pour drinks;

3. To make tea for mothers.

Up to your child's third or fourth birthday you will probably find that the party will go better if the mothers stay and help. Make a nice big pot of tea for them, and include the numbers of mothers in your estimate of the required size of birthday cake, as they will probably all like to have a slice. Once the children reach the age of four or five, parents will merely act as chauffeurs, ferrying their children to and from parties. But try, if you can, to organize a cup of tea or a drink for them when they collect their children, to make them feel welcome too. In the summer make a big jug of iced coffee or tea, which you can make in advance. Keep in the fridge during the party, and bring it out as required. (See the section on drinks for recipes.) Another good idea is to buy a big 5 litre bottle of wine (put it in the fridge before the party if it is white wine). Have the glasses arranged ready in a corner and offer one to each parent as they arrive to collect their offspring. Have one yourself too!

Metric conversions are approximate, so stick to either metric or imperial measures in any one recipe.

Starters

Start the tea with an individual bowl of jelly or ice cream for each child. For very small children, it is a good idea to make an egg custard to go with jelly. In this way the children get some sensible nourishment before the rest of the party food. All the jelly recipes can be made the day before the party.

We give lots of ice cream cake recipes (pages 73–75), but if you are not making an ice cream cake, then you can start the party with a serving of ice cream. Preparing the bowls of ice cream should be a last-minute job, but if you've room in your freezer, you can do it in advance, putting the bowls of ice cream on a tray and the tray in the freezer until required.

If you are having a summer party, where the children can run around the garden, you can finish tea by giving each child an ice cream cornet with a chocolate flake (obtainable in bulk from Bejams) to be eaten out of doors. (NB, this is *not* recommended for indoor parties!)

Egg Custard and Jelly

Serves 8–10

1 tablespoon cornflour
1 tablespoon sugar
1 pint (570 ml) milk
3 eggs
1 packet jelly
Hundreds and thousands

Mix the cornflour and sugar in a bowl with 2 tablespoons of cold milk. Add the eggs, and beat until the mixture is smooth. Heat the rest of the milk in a saucepan until almost boiling, then pour gently over the mixture in the bowl, stirring all the time. Pour back into the saucepan, and cook very gently, stirring all the time, so that the mixture thickens, but does not go lumpy. When it is thick enough to coat the back of a spoon, take it off the heat and continue to stir until fairly cool. Pour about 2 tablespoons of the custard into the bottom of each dish and leave to set.

Make up the jelly according to the instructions on the packet and leave it to cool. Just before it begins to set, pour it gently over the custard in each dish, and leave to set. Before serving sprinkle coloured hundreds and thousands over the top (not before or they melt into the jelly).

Fruit Salad Jelly

Make up the jelly according to the instructions on the packet, but minus ½ pint (300 ml) cold water. Add a can of fruit salad, including the juice, to the jelly and mix well. Pour gently into individual dishes and leave to set.

Multicoloured Jelly

A good way to serve jelly is to make two jellies of different colours in separate bowls – for instance, red and green, or yellow and purple. When they are set, chop them up roughly with a knife, and spoon them into the dishes with the darker colour at the bottom. This makes a pretty sparkly effect. If you are adding decorations, such as hundreds and thousands, do it at the last minute, just before you serve up, otherwise they will melt and the colours will run, and look very sad.

Jelly Froth

Serves 8–10

1 packet jelly
Small can evaporated milk
Hundreds and thousands

Dissolve the jelly in a bowl, in ½ pint (300 ml) boiling water, stirring all the time. Put in the fridge until the jelly begins to set. Whisk the evaporated milk, until the mixture is thick and frothy. Add to the jelly and whisk again. Pour into individual jelly cases, and put back in the fridge to set.

Decorate with hundreds and thousands or other decorations just before serving.

Simple Sundae

Put two scoops of different coloured ice cream into each dish, sprinkle with hundreds and thousands, or stick a glacé cherry, Smartie or chocolate button on to the top of each scoop, and serve immediately.

Chocolate Lemon Cups

Makes 12

A slightly more complicated recipe, but older children will find it very sophisticated. The chocolate cases can be made in advance and kept in the fridge, but keep the paper cases around them until required.

For the cases
8 oz (225 g) plain chocolate or chocolate cake covering
Knob of butter
12 paper cases

For the jelly
1 packet lemon jelly
1 small can evaporated milk

Melt the chocolate with the butter over a very gentle heat, stirring all the time. Pour some gently into each paper case, spooning it up the sides, so that the chocolate makes quite a thick layer. Put in the fridge to set.

Make up the jelly in a bowl with ½ pint (300 ml) boiling water, and stir until dissolved. Put the bowl in the fridge until it has almost set, then add the evaporated milk and whisk until the mixture is frothy.

Carefully remove the paper cases from the chocolate cups, and spoon the jelly into each cup. Return to the fridge to set. Decorate with chocolate vermicelli or a chocolate button just before serving.

Cat's Whiskers' Ice Cream

Put a layer of chocolate ice cream into each dish and make domes for the cats' heads by using a scoop of vanilla ice cream. Stick two chocolate buttons on top of the head for ears, use sultanas to make the eyes, nose and mouth, then break Matchmakers in half and stick in three on either side of the mouth to form whiskers. Serve immediately.

Sailing Ships Ice Cream and Peaches

Place a canned peach half flat side up in the bottom of each bowl. Put a scoop of chocolate ice cream on top, and stick in a triangular sail, made by cutting wafer biscuits in half, diagonally.

Knickerbocker Glory

Serves 12

1 packet red jelly
1 packet yellow jelly
1 can mandarin oranges, drained
1 can pineapple, drained and chopped
1¾ pint (1 litre) block ice cream

Make up the two jellies following the instructions on the packet, using the juice from the canned fruit in the pint of liquid. Mix the fruit and spoon it into ten tall sundae glasses. Chop the jelly when set, and add in layers. Top with a scoop of ice cream. Decorate with hundreds and thousands, and serve at once.

Savouries

There is no point in making large amounts of ordinary sandwiches, but children do seem to love savouries nowadays, and it is a good idea to make some extra special party sandwiches that look as appetizing as they taste. You can make these in advance and freeze them. Take out of the freezer 2 hours before the party. If the sandwiches have not been frozen before, you can also freeze the leftovers. Never freeze sandwiches containing hard-boiled egg.

Single Deckers

These freeze well, are simplicity itself to make, and small children love them.

Small brown or white loaf
Softened butter
Hundreds and thousands
Chocolate vermicelli

Slice the bread into ½ inch (1·25 cm) thick slices. Cut off the crusts. Butter the slices and cut into neat squares, or use pastry cutters to cut into shapes (which means a lot of wasted bread). Stand the squares on a wire rack over a sheet of greaseproof paper, and sprinkle with hundreds and thousands. Pick up the paper under the rack and re-use the hundreds and thousands that have fallen through. Repeat the procedure using the chocolate vermicelli, and arrange them alternately in the serving dish.

Pinwheels

See photograph on page 76.

This makes about 25 sandwiches, which can be made in advance and frozen.

1 small loaf of brown bread
Softened butter
5 slices cooked ham, thinly sliced
3 oz (75 g) packet of Philadelphia cream
   cheese or Dairylea cheese (for very
   young children)

Put the loaf in the freezer for 2 hours, as this makes it much easier to cut thinly. Take it out of the freezer, cut away the rounded crust from the top, and trim away the side crusts and the ends. Cut five thin slices lengthways from the loaf, and butter them. If there is any of the loaf left, use it for making Single Decker Sandwiches. Put a slice of ham on top of the butter, and then spread cream cheese thinly over the ham. Roll up lengthways, and wrap tightly in foil, or cling film, and chill for 2 hours in the fridge. Take out of the fridge, and cut each roll into ½ inch (1·25 cm) slices – you should be able to cut at least five from each roll.

If you don't have any ham, use Marmite or Bovril. Spread it over the butter, and then spread the cheese on top. This way the colour does not run into the bread.

Triple Decker Sandwiches

This makes 20 sandwiches, which can be made in advance, and frozen (all except for those filled with egg).

Small loaf of brown bread
Softened butter

Suggested fillings
Thinly sliced ham
Sliced cheese
Cream cheese with a little salt and pepper
Hard boiled eggs, chopped up with salad cream, or softened butter, with salt and pepper (do not freeze)
Cream cheese and chopped dates, mixed
Cream cheese and chopped apple or pineapple, mixed
Cream cheese coloured with a little tomato ketchup
Sandwich spread
Marmite or Bovril
Peanut butter

Put the loaf in the freezer for 2 hours, as this makes it easier to cut. Take out of the freezer, cut away the rounded crust from the top, the side crusts, and the ends, and slice lengthways. Take three of the slices, butter them and spread two of them with two of the suggested fillings. Place one slice on the other and press the third slice firmly down on top. Wrap in foil or cling film, and chill for 2 hours. Repeat with the remaining slices of bread, either using the same fillings, or varying them. Take out of the fridge, and cut downwards into half-inch slices. You should be able to cut ten sandwiches from each section.

Bridge Roll Boats

See photograph on page 76.

Miniature bridge rolls
Some thinly sliced ham
Lettuce
Cocktail sticks

Fillings
Slice of cheese, slice of tomato
Hard boiled eggs chopped up with salad cream or softened butter
Cream cheese and chopped dates mixed
Cream cheese, chopped apple or pineapple mixed
Sandwich spread

Allow one or two boats per child. This will be plenty as they are quite filling. Bridge rolls are much easier to cut and butter if they are frozen. Cut each bridge roll in half, butter the halves and put a layer of ham over the butter, followed by the chosen filling. To make the sail, cut or tear out a triangular piece of lettuce, push the cocktail stick through the lettuce in two places to hold it upright, and then push the end of a stick into the centre of each bridge roll.

Cheese Straws

You can make these in the traditional straw shape, or use cutters in the shape of animals, ducks, gingerbread men, and so on to make amusing shapes for the children. Make them up to a week in advance, but store in an airtight tin.

Oven Temperature: 350°F, 180°C, Gas Mark 5

4 oz (110 g) plain flour
1 teaspoon salt
2 oz (50 g) butter
2 oz (50 g) Cheddar cheese, grated
1 egg yolk
1 tablespoon cold water

Sift flour and salt together, and rub in the butter to give a texture of fine breadcrumbs. Stir in the cheese and egg yolk, and add enough cold water to give a stiff dough, but be careful not to add too much. Roll the pastry thinly, and if you are making straws trim into 8 inch (20 cm) squares. Put on a greased baking tray, and cut into straws, 2 inches (5 cm) long and ¼ inch (6 mm) wide, separating them gently with the knife. If you are using cutters, cut out the shapes before you put them on the tray. You can use up the leftovers by re-rolling them, but this will produce a slightly tougher result. Bake in the centre of the oven for 10–15 minutes, until golden.

Sausages

Children love sausages, and you should allow three or four per child. Cook them the day before the party, and put in the fridge when cool. If you can buy small cocktail sausages, then do so, but if not you can make your own.

To make your own, buy chipolata sausages, and before you cook them, untwist the skin and squeeze each sausage gently in half, and re-twist. Do not cut them apart until cooked. Put them on a tray in the oven with a little cooking fat at 350°F, 180°C, or Gas Mark 5, for about 20 minutes. Drain off the fat, leave to drain on kitchen roll, and then separate with a sharp knife or scissors. Pierce each with a cocktail stick and arrange on two suitable dishes, so that you have one at either end of the table (or see next recipe).

Sausage and Cheese Party Piece

See photograph on page 76.

Cooked sausages (see above)
½ inch (1·25 cm) cubes of Cheddar cheese
2 oranges
Coloured cocktail sticks

Cut a small slice off one end of each orange to make a firm base, and place the oranges, cut ends down, on small saucers. Stick the sausages and the cubes of cheese onto the cocktail sticks, and then push the sticks into the oranges, spreading them evenly around. These make very pretty table decorations, as well as being extremely popular to eat.

Baby Sausage Rolls

Makes 20
Oven Temperature: 350°F, 180°C,
Gas Mark 5

The pastry
2 oz (50 g) butter (but do not cut it off the
   block)
3 oz (75 g) self-raising flour
1 dessertspoon water
or
8 oz (225 g) packet Jusrol Flaky Pastry

Filling
4 oz (110 g) sausage meat
A little milk

Make these the day before the party. Use a block of very cold butter, or better still put it in the freezer for 2 hours. Unwrap one end of the block and mark off a 2 oz (50 g) section. Sift a little of the flour into a bowl, and with a coarse grater grate the butter on top of the flour. Then add more flour, and continue until both are used up. Mix together very gently, with a metal spoon, until the mixture resembles fine breadcrumbs, then add water to mix. The finished mixture should feel light and require no kneading. Roll out into a rectangle on a floured board, again very gently, and cut into two strips lengthways. Divide the sausage meat in two halves, and roll with your hands into two sausages, the same length as the pastry. Brush the long edges of the pastry with milk, and lay the roll of sausage meat down the length of the pastry and bring the edges up to the centre to cover the sausage meat. Press the edges firmly together, making an indented edge with your finger tips, and brush the pastry with milk. Place on a greased baking tray

and cut into rolls, 1 inch (2·5 cm) long, with the knife, and cook for 15 minutes. Reduce the oven temperature to 300°F, 170°C, Gas Mark 4, and cook for a further 10 minutes, but don't let them get too brown. They should rise well and be deep gold to light brown in colour.

Miniature Cheese Scones

Makes 28

These can be made a day or two before the party and kept in an airtight tin.

Oven Temperature: 350°F, 180°C,
Gas Mark 5

4 oz (110 g) self-raising flour
1 teaspoon salt
1 oz (25 g) butter
2 oz (50 g) Cheddar cheese, grated
A little milk

Stir the flour and salt together and rub in the fat, until the mixture resembles fine breadcrumbs. Add the cheese and enough milk to make a soft dough, but be careful not to make it too slack. Roll it out to a thickness of about ½ inch (1·25 cm), or pat it out with your hands, and cut it into rounds with a 1 inch (2·5 cm) diameter pastry cutter. If you do not have a small enough cutter, use the well-washed plastic top of an aerosol spray or any bottle top with a sharp edge (a Stergene bottle top is ideal). Place on a greased baking tray, brush the tops with milk, and cook for about 10 minutes. You can cut them in half and spread the halves with butter before serving.

Small cakes and biscuits

Gingerbread Biscuits

Makes 20

These can be made several days in advance if kept in an airtight tin.

Oven Temperature: 350°F, 180°C, Gas Mark 4

2 oz (50 g) butter
2 oz (50 g) sugar
4½ oz (125 g) plain flour
½ teaspoon bicarbonate of soda
1 teaspoon ground ginger
Warmed syrup

Cream the butter with the sugar until soft. Add the dry ingredients, mixed with a little warmed syrup to make a dough mixture. Having lightly kneaded this, flour a board and roll it out. If you wish, you could make gingerbread men (see following recipe), but these tend to be very large for smaller children to eat, so we suggest that you use instead your duck or dog cutters. Place your shapes on to a greased tray, and decorate with currants for eyes, etc. Bake for 10–15 minutes and allow to cool before placing on a wire rack.

Gingerbread Men

See photograph on page 76.

On page 40 we suggest that these make lovely presents for the children to take home, even if they are a little too large for younger children to eat at the tea table. Follow the previous recipe, and cut out the men with your man-shaped cutter. Cook and leave to cool as above. Decorate in one of several ways:
1. Use chocolate polka dots for the eyes, nose, mouth and buttons, and stick them on with a touch of slightly whisked egg white.
2. Make up a small quantity of icing and pipe on eyes, nose, mouth and buttons.
3. Use a very thin nozzle with a piping bag, or a strong paper or plastic bag with a tiny snip off one corner. Pipe (if you are very clever) each child's name across the front of each gingerbread man. Have a few un-named ones for spares in case of breakages. If the whole name is a bit difficult, and it does require practice, then why not just try a big initial for each child? If you do break any of them, don't despair. Use egg white as glue – it works a treat.

Coloured Meringue Drops

See photograph on page 76.

Makes 30

There is a certain mystique about making meringues, and some cooks feel reluctant to try them, but meringues are actually very easy and if you follow the instructions carefully you should have no trouble at all. Meringue making has been enormously simplified since the introduction of silicone paper: simply lift the meringues off the paper – they will never stick – and the paper can be brushed down and re-used a number of times.

You can make your meringues up to two weeks in advance, but they must be stored in an airtight tin.

Oven Temperature: 180°F, 90°C, Gas Mark ¾

2 egg whites
4 oz (110 g) caster sugar
Few drops green and pink colouring

These coloured meringues must be cooked very slowly indeed, so that they do not change colour, but remain a fresh pink, green or white. Whisk the egg whites with an electric beater until *very* stiff. Add 2 oz (50 g) of the sugar and continue to whisk until mixture holds a peak. Gently fold in the remaining sugar. Put a tiny blob of meringue under each corner of the paper on the baking trays to hold the paper down. Take a very small teaspoonful of meringue and, with another teaspoon, slide the mixture on to the tray, making a small round meringue. Do this until you have made 10 meringues and have used about one-third of the mixture. Put half the remaining mixture into a separate bowl, add a few drops of the pink colouring and mix gently until the colour is even. Make another 10 meringues using the two spoons. Colour the last part of the mixture with a few drops of green colouring, and spoon on to the remaining tray. Cook near the bottom of the oven for 40 minutes. When they are firm to the touch, turn off the oven and leave them until they are completely cold.

Chocolate Meringues

Makes 30

If you are worried about making coloured meringues because you feel that yours go brown however slowly you cook them, then why not try chocolate meringues. They can also be made well in advance.

Oven Temperature: 180°F, 90°C, Gas Mark ¾

2 egg whites
4 oz (110 g) caster sugar
1 tablespoon cocoa

Whisk the egg whites with an electric beater until they are stiff. Add 2 oz (50 g) of the sugar and continue to whisk until the mixture holds a peak. Gently fold in the cocoa and the remaining sugar. Spoon the meringue mixture on to the trays and cook as in the previous recipe.

2 3 4 Shortbread

Makes 30

This recipe never fails, and gets its name from the proportions of the ingredients. It keeps well in an airtight tin.

Oven Temperature: 300°F, 150°C, Gas Mark 2

2 oz (50 g) butter
3 oz (75 g) caster sugar
4 oz (110 g) plain flour

Grease a baking tin, approximately 8 inches (20 cm) square. Put the butter into a mixing bowl. Rub in the sifted sugar and flour until the mixture resembles fine breadcrumbs. Then gently knead it together with your hands, and pat out into the greased tin. Cook for 10 minutes. The mixture should not change colour. Take out of the oven and cut into thin fingers. Leave in tin until cool.

Shortbread Shapes

These are nice to make if you have cutters to make ducks, fish and other nice shapes. The man-shaped cutter makes biscuits that are a little too large for small children, so save it until your children are older. Follow the recipe for Shortbread Faces, but use your different shapes. Draw the duck's eye and wings and the fishes' eyes and fins with icing as before, and add chocolate polka dots for the eyes.

Shortbread Faces

See photograph on page 76.

Makes 35

You can make these a few days in advance, but ice them the day before the party.

Oven Temperature: 300°F, 150°C, Gas Mark 2

4 oz (110 g) softened butter or margarine
2 oz (50 g) caster sugar
6 oz (175 g) plain flour
Icing
3 oz (75 g) icing sugar
1 or 2 tablespoons boiling water
Pink colouring
Chocolate polka dots (optional)

Put the butter into a mixing bowl. Add the sugar and beat well, then add the flour. Gently knead with your hands into a soft ball. Pat on to a floured board and roll it out lightly and thinly to about $\frac{1}{8}$ inch (3 mm) thick. Use a small round cutter, about $1\frac{1}{2}$ inch (3·75 cm) in diameter. Cut out as many biscuits as you can, re-roll the leftovers, and cut these out also. Place the biscuits on a greased baking sheet and bake towards the top of the oven for 10–15 minutes, until pale gold. Cool.

To make the icing, add the water and colouring to the icing sugar, and mix well. The mixture should be a little more stiff than you think is right as it will soften when you hold it. Put the icing into a paper bag, cut a very small hole in one corner and pipe a face on to each biscuit (when they are quite cold) with small blobs of icing for eyes and nose, and a nice smiley line for a mouth. Place a polka dot on each of the eye blobs – children cannot resist them.

Little Gems

See photograph on page 76.

Makes 24

If you like you can use this recipe to make up half of the quantity Little Gems and make the rest into Butterflies (see following recipe). Both make very pretty little cakes, but young children may need a little help in taking off the paper cases. You could make these two days before the party, and ice them the day before.

Oven Temperature: 350°F, 180°C, Gas Mark 4

4 oz (110 g) butter or soft margarine
4 oz (110 g) caster sugar
2 eggs
4 oz (110 g) self-raising flour
24 petit fours cases

Icing

4 oz (110 g) icing sugar
1 or 2 tablespoons boiling water
Few drops pink colouring
Mixed decorations, including halved glacé cherries, chocolate buttons, Smarties, hundreds and thousands, Jelly Tots, etc.

Preheat the oven, and place the paper cases on a baking sheet. Beat the butter and sugar together until pale and smooth. Beat the eggs in a separate bowl and add to the mixture, a little at a time, beating well between each addition. Sieve the flour into the bowl from quite a height to help lighten it, and fold in with a metal spoon. (Add a few drops of milk if the mixture is a little stiff.) Spoon the mixture into the paper cases, filling each case about two-thirds full. Cook in the centre of the oven for about 15 minutes, until the cakes are golden brown. Remove from oven and leave to cool.

Make up the icing so that it is quite stiff, adding the boiling water very gradually. With a teaspoon spoon the icing on to half of the cakes, putting the decorations in place immediately. Colour the remaining icing pink and spoon on to the rest of the cakes, again adding your decorations at once.

Butterflies

Makes 24

Again small children may need a little help in taking off the paper cases. You can make them two days before the party, and ice them the day before – perhaps at the same time as the cake.

Oven Temperature: 350°F, 180°C, Gas Mark 4

4 oz (110 g) butter or soft margarine
4 oz (110 g) caster sugar
2 eggs
4 oz (110 g) self-raising flour
24 petit fours cases

Icing

1 oz (25 g) softened butter
2 oz (50 g) icing sugar
2 or 3 drops vanilla essence

Make the Butterflies in exactly the same way as Little Gems.

To make the butter icing, cream the butter with the icing sugar and beat until smooth. Cut off the tops of the cakes, and cut each top in half. Put a teaspoonful of butter icing on the top of each cake and stick the two pieces on as wings into the butter icing.

Chocolate Crispies

See photograph on page 76.

Makes 20

These will keep fresh for several days in an airtight tin.

Oven Temperature: 200°F, 100°C, Gas Mark 2

2 oz (50 g) cornflakes or rice krispies
6 oz (175 g) plain chocolate
1 oz (25 g) butter or margarine

Spread the cornflakes over a shallow baking tray, and put into the bottom of the oven for 10 minutes. Remove from the oven and leave to cool. When they are cool crumble them up until fairly small. They should be very crisp. Melt the chocolate and butter over a gentle heat (do *not* add water as this will make the cornflakes go soggy). Stir in the cornflakes and shape the mixture into small conical heaps on a greased baking tray, and leave to set.

Coconut Pyramids

Makes 30

You can make these two or three days before the party.

Oven Temperature: 250°F, 120°C, Gas Mark 1

2 egg whites
8 oz (225 g) caster sugar
4 oz (110 g) desiccated coconut
Few drops of pink colouring

Whisk the egg whites until very stiff. Whisk in half the caster sugar, again until very stiff. Gently fold in the remaining sugar and the coconut. Shape half the mixture into small pyramids, on a greased baking sheet. Add a few drops of pink colouring to the remaining mixture, and shape into small pink pyramids. Cook for 30 minutes at the bottom of the oven.

Scrumptious Coconut Bars

Makes 16

Make two or three days in advance.

Oven Temperature: 350°F, 180°C, Gas Mark 4

4 oz (110 g) self-raising flour
4 oz (110 g) caster sugar
4 oz (110 g) desiccated coconut
2 oz (50 g) cornflakes
5 oz (150 g) butter
Icing
2 tablespoons boiling water
2 teaspoons instant coffee
6 oz (175 g) icing sugar

Mix the dry ingredients in a bowl. Melt the butter, pour over dry ingredients and mix well. Press into a greased baking tin. Cook for 15 minutes until golden brown.

Meanwhile, to make the icing, pour the boiling water over the coffee and stir into the icing sugar. Add a little more water if necessary. Pour the icing over the biscuits as soon as you take them out of the oven. Leave to cool and cut into small bars.

Chocolate Peppermint Creams

Makes 30

Make these up to a week before the party.

4 oz (110 g) plain chocolate
4 oz (110 g) margarine
4 tablespoons golden syrup
Few drops peppermint essence
Petit fours *paper cases*
Coloured hundreds and thousands

Melt the chocolate over a gentle heat. Cream the margarine with the syrup and beat in the melted chocolate. Add the drops of peppermint essence and mix well. Pour into *petit fours* cases, decorate the tops with hundreds and thousands, and leave to set. For very small children, peel off the cases before you serve the cakes.

Coconut Drops

Makes 20

Make these the day before the party.

Oven Temperature: 250°F, 120°C, Gas Mark 1

1 small can condensed milk
8 oz (225 g) desiccated coconut
Few drops pink and green colouring

Mix the condensed milk and coconut. Divide into three equal parts; leave one white and colour the others pink and green. Shape with a teaspoon into small moulds on a greased baking tray, and cook for about 30 minutes at the bottom of the oven. It is important that they do not go brown as they cook or the colouring will be spoiled.

Chocolate Crunch Cakes

Makes 30

Make two or three days in advance, and keep in the fridge.

8 oz (225 g) plain chocolate
1 egg yolk
2 oz (50 g) unsalted peanuts, chopped
2 oz (50 g) rice krispies
30 paper cases

Melt the chocolate over a very gentle heat, and stir in the egg yolk. Then stir in the dry ingredients, until they are well mixed. Put teaspoonfuls of the mixture into paper cases and leave to set.

Date Fingers

Makes 28

These are best when freshly made so try to make them no sooner than the day before the party.

Oven Temperature: 350°F, 180°C, Gas Mark 4

1 oz (25 g) butter
8 oz (225 g) chopped dates
1 tablespoon sugar
1 tablespoon self-raising flour
1 egg

Melt the butter and stir in all the other ingredients. Press the mixture into a greased baking tin. Don't worry if it looks like a sticky mess at this stage. Cook for 30 minutes and cut into fingers when cool.

Peppermint Squares

See photograph on page 76.

Makes 30

These are delicious, but rather rich, so keep them small. You can make them a day or two before the party.

Oven Temperature: 350°F, 180°C, Gas Mark 4

2 oz (50 g) cornflakes
3 oz (75 g) butter or margarine
2 oz (50 g) plain flour
2 oz (50 g) desiccated coconut
2 oz (50 g) sugar
½ teaspoon peppermint essence
Icing
4 oz (110 g) butter or margarine
8 oz (225 g) icing sugar
½ teaspoon peppermint essence
Chocolate buttons to decorate

Lightly crush the cornflakes. Melt the butter in a saucepan over a gentle heat and stir in the cornflakes, flour, coconut, sugar and peppermint essence. Press into a well-greased baking tin – use a fork – so that the mixture is evenly and thinly spread (not more than ¼ inch or 6 mm thick). Cook for 20 minutes until light gold in colour.

Make up the icing and when the biscuit mixture is cold, spread on top and roughen the surface with a fork. Cut into 1 inch (2·5 cm) squares, and press a chocolate button on to the centre of each square.

Chocolate Truffles

See photograph on page 76.

Makes 40

You can make these two or three days in advance, but keep them in the fridge.

4 oz (110 g) plain sweet biscuits
2 oz (50 g) digestive biscuits
3½ oz (85 g) butter or margarine
1 oz (25 g) caster sugar
3 tablespoons golden syrup
2 oz (50 g) cocoa
Chocolate vermicelli
Coloured hundreds and thousands
Petit fours *cases*

Crush the biscuits roughly with a rolling pin. Cream together the butter, sugar and golden syrup. Beat in the sifted cocoa and work in the crushed biscuits, mixing well. If the mixture is too soft, leave in the fridge for 30 minutes. When sufficiently firm, wash your hands well, and take teaspoonful size pieces of the dough, and roll between your hands to make neat round balls. Pour some coloured hundreds and thousands into a small bowl, and taking half the truffles roll each in the bowl until well covered. Place in *petit fours* cases to set. Roll the remaining half in chocolate vermicelli in the same way, put into cases, and arrange the truffles alternately on the serving dish. Put in the fridge to harden.

Chocolate Shortbread Treat

Makes 32

These are at their best when freshly made, but will keep well if necessary.

Oven Temperature: 350°F, 180°C, or Gas Mark 4

Shortbread base
6 oz (175 g) flour
1 oz (25 g) caster sugar
4 oz (110 g) butter

Filling
4 oz (110 g) butter
4 oz (110 g) soft brown sugar
2 level tablespoons golden syrup
1 small can condensed milk

Icing
8 oz (225 g) plain dessert chocolate
1 oz (25 g) butter

Grease the baking tin. Sift the flour into a bowl, add the sugar and rub in the butter until the mixture looks like breadcrumbs. Knead it into a ball and press it well into the tin. Cook for 15 minutes. Leave to cool in the tin.

To make the filling, put all the ingredients into a saucepan and stir over a gentle heat until the sugar has dissolved. Bring to the boil and, stirring continuously, boil gently for 7 minutes. Take off the heat and beat well, and pour on to the shortbread base. Allow to cool before adding the icing.

To make the icing, cut the chocolate up roughly and melt over a very gentle heat with the butter. Spread it evenly over the filling. When the chocolate is quite cold, cut the mixture into 32 squares.

Julianna's Uncooked Cookies

Makes 36

Make a day or two in advance, and keep in the fridge.

8 oz (225 g) sweet tea biscuits
2 tablespoons golden syrup
4 oz (110 g) butter
4 oz (110 g) sugar

Put the biscuits into a plastic bag, fasten the top and crush with a rolling pin. Dissolve the golden syrup and butter, mix in the crushed biscuits and the sugar, and press with a fork into a greased baking tray to set. When firm cut into fingers.

Cherry Crisps

Makes 30

Don't make this recipe too far in advance – a day or two if possible, and keep in an airtight tin.

2 oz (50 g) butter
2 oz (50 g) sugar
4 oz (110 g) dates, chopped
2 oz (50 g) cherries, chopped
2 oz (50 g) rice krispies

Melt the butter and sugar in a saucepan over a low heat. Add the chopped dates and cherries. Stir in the (very crisp) rice krispies and form into small pyramids on a greased baking tray. Leave to set.

5 6 7 Flapjacks

So called because of the quantities used! The easiest never-fail recipe there is. Flapjacks keep very well, for weeks if necessary, but are at their best when fresh. Keep in an airtight tin.

Oven Temperature: 350°F, 180°C, Gas Mark 4

5 oz (150 g) butter or margarine
6 oz (175 g) granulated sugar
7 oz (200 g) porridge oats

Melt the butter over a low heat, with the sugar (you will find that the sugar will not really dissolve, but don't worry, it's not meant to!). Stir in the porridge oats and pour into a shallow well-greased tray. Cook in the centre of the oven for 20 minutes, until golden brown. Remove from oven and mark into narrow fingers. Leave to cool in the tin.

Uncooked Chocolate Cake

Make two or three days in advance, and keep in the fridge.

4 oz (110 g) butter
4 oz (110 g) dark chocolate
2 tablespoons golden syrup
8 oz (225 g) digestive biscuits

Melt the butter, chocolate and syrup – do not allow to boil – then take off the heat. Put the biscuits into a plastic bag, fasten at the top, and crush with a rolling pin, until the biscuits are in small even crumbs. Mix with the other ingredients, and press into a greased baking tray. Smooth the surface and leave to set, then cut into squares, as many as you like.

Drinks

Very small children (one to four year olds) are perfectly happy with a big jug of orangeade, but the older children would appreciate a little variety. They love, needless to say, Coca-Cola, fizzy lemonade etc, but they also love the fresh taste of home-made drinks, with their ice cubes, little bits of fruit, pretty colours and so on. If you are having a big party, why not compromise: buy some ready-made drinks and make a fizzy orange or apple punch as well. If you are having a small party, or special teatime treat for about six children, then try some of the more adventurous milk or ice cream shakes. They are delicious as well as nourishing.

The first eight children's recipes in this section will serve about ten, depending on the weather and spillages, but keep some orange squash or fizzy lemonade in reserve. The milk shakes will serve about six.

Iced Coffee *For the mothers.*

Serves 8

3 tablespoons instant coffee
Sugar to taste (about 2 tablespoons)
¼ pint (150 ml) boiling water
2 pints (1 litre) cold milk
Ice cubes
Scoops of ice cream (optional)

Put the coffee and sugar in a large jug, add the boiling water and stir well. Then add the cold milk and ice cubes. Keep in the fridge until needed. Put a scoop of ice cream into each glass and pour the coffee over it.

Iced Tea *For the mothers.*

Serves 8

4 large teaspoons tea (half China tea if you
have it)
1 pint (570 ml) boiling water
1 pint (570 ml) cold water
Ice cubes
8 slices of lemon
Sugar (optional)

Make a strong pot of tea with the boiling water. Allow to brew for 5 minutes, then strain into a large jug and add the cold water and lemon slices. When tea is cold add ice cubes and keep in fridge. Offer sugar individually.

Home-made Lemonade

4 lemons
4 tablespoons sugar
3 pints (1·5 litres) boiling water
10 ice cubes

Cut the lemons into quarters. Put them with the sugar into a heat-resistant jug. Pour on the boiling water and leave to stand for 30 minutes. Strain, cool, add the ice cubes, and serve.

Home-made Orangeade

Follow the recipe for lemonade as above. When it is cool, squeeze the juice of four oranges into the lemonade, add the ice cubes and serve.

Home-made Blender Lemonade

4 thin skinned lemons
4 tablespoons sugar
10 ice cubes
3 pints (1·5 litres) cold water

Cut the lemons into quarters. Put all the ingredients, reserving 2 pints (1 litre) of water and 5 ice cubes, into the blender and blend for 10 seconds. Strain, add remaining water and ice cubes and serve.

Right: Some colourful party drinks.

Fizzy Apple Punch

½ pint (300 ml) bottle concentrated apple
  juice
2 pints (1 litre) soda water
2 pints (1 litre) ginger ale
2 eating apples (red if possible)

Chill all the ingredients (except the apples)
for 2 hours. Quarter and core the apples,
but do not peel them, and cut the quarters
into small chunks. Put into a large jug. Pour
over the other ingredients and serve.

Fizzy Apricot Punch

1 × 10 oz (275 g) can apricots (stoned)
2 lemons
3 pints (1·5 litres) fizzy lemonade

Chill all the ingredients for at least 2 hours.
Cut the lemons into quarters, and put into a
blender with the apricots. Blend for 20
seconds. Strain into a serving jug, and mix
well with ½ pint (300 ml) lemonade.
Add the rest of the lemonade, and serve.

Fizzy Orange Punch I

1 large carton frozen orange juice
  concentrate
3 pints (1·5 litres) fizzy lemonade
10 ice cubes
A few slices of orange

Dilute the frozen orange juice with ½ pint
(300 ml) lemonade. When it is well mixed
pour into serving jug, add the rest of the
lemonade, the ice cubes and the slices of
orange, and serve.

Fizzy Orange Punch II

1 pint (570 ml) pure orange juice (tinned or
  bottled)
2 pints (1 litre) tonic water
10 ice cubes
A few orange slices

Chill the ingredients in the fridge for at
least 2 hours. Pour the orange juice into a
jug. Mix well with ½ pint (300 ml) of the
tonic water. Add the rest of the tonic water,
the ice cubes, the slices of orange, and
serve.

Banana Whiz

2 bananas
1 egg
2 pints (1 litre) cold milk
1 tablespoon sugar

Peel the bananas, chop, and put in the
blender. Break the egg into the blender,
and add the other ingredients, reserving 1
pint (570 ml) of milk. Blend for 20 seconds
until foaming. Add the remaining milk. Pour
into tall glasses and serve with straws.

Cola Surprise

3 pints (1·5 litres) Coca-Cola or Pepsi-Cola
Small carton of ice cream

Spoon or scoop the ice cream into each
serving glass. Pour the Cola over and
serve.

Chocolate Banana Shake

2 bananas
2 pints (1 litre) cold milk
2 heaped tablespoons drinking chocolate
*   or 1 tablespoon each cocoa and sugar*

Peel the bananas, chop, and put into the blender. Add the other ingredients, reserving 1 pint (570 ml) of milk, and blend for 20 seconds until foamy. Add remaining milk. Pour into tall glasses and serve with straws.

Pineapple Dream

1 × 10 oz (275 g) can pineapple chunks
2 pints (1 litre) cold milk
Vanilla ice cream

Put the pineapple, the juice and 1 pint (570 ml) milk into the liquidizer, and blend for 20 seconds. Add remaining milk. Pour into serving glasses and top with a scoopful of vanilla ice cream. Serve with straws.

Blackcurrant Delight

5 tablespoons Ribena
2 pints (1 litre) cold milk
Vanilla ice cream

Mix the Ribena and milk together. Pour into tall glasses. Top with a scoop of vanilla ice cream and serve with straws.

Peppermint Delight

Few drops peppermint essence
Few drops green colouring
1 tablespoon sugar
2 pints (1 litre) cold milk
Soft ice cream

Add the peppermint essence, the green colouring and the sugar to the cold milk, and stir well. Pour into tall glasses and top with a scoop of ice cream.

Apricot Delight

1 × 10 oz (275 g) can apricots (stoned)
1 tablespoon sugar
2 pints (1 litre) milk
6 ice cubes

Put all the ingredients into a blender, reserving 1 pint (570 ml) milk, and blend for 20 seconds. Add remaining milk. Pour into tall glasses and serve with straws.

Raspberry Soda

8 oz (225 g) fresh or frozen raspberries
2 pints (1 litre) milk
Small bottle tonic water
Small block of Raspberry Ripple ice cream

Partially defrost the frozen raspberries. Put the raspberries and 1 pint (570 ml) milk into a blender and blend for 20 seconds. Strain. Add remaining milk and tonic water. Pour into serving glasses. Top with a scoop of ice cream.

4. PARTY GAMES

The most important consideration, when planning what amusements to provide to stop the children being either shy, bored, or running riot through your house, is to base your choice of games on (a) the ages of your guests, and (b) the size of your house (or garden if you are planning a summer party). Make a list of the games which you think would be suitable and plan a rough timetable – it is amazing how quickly the children, especially the older ones, can get through the games. Keep the games coming thick and fast and don't allow gaps to develop between them.

For babies' parties just have lots of toys around – with the exception of your child's pride and joy, as tinies can be very possessive. Play nursery records and tapes to clap and jump to. Really these parties are a super excuse for a special tea with your friends and their children – and why not!

This chapter is divided into two parts. The first contains games suitable for the very young, but there are inevitably some games which overlap and continue to be popular with older children. The second part concentrates on the older group. We have tried to organize the sections chronologically, starting with the games aimed at involving everybody at the beginning of the party, while guests are arriving, continuing with something energetic before tea, followed by quieter games suitable for immediately afterwards, and finally suggesting a medley of ideas to draw the party to a conclusion on a high note. There are ideas for outdoor games for fine weather parties. You will find that little girls are happy to play party games longer than the boys – even at ten, girls are content to 'pass the parcel' although with forfeits, whereas boys would consider it 'sissy'!

It is a super treat for your guests to be given little prizes for winning games. The smallest token is quite sufficient – a pencil, sweet or marble (but not marbles for the under fives). Always have a few extra 'spare' prizes, in case of a draw or other problem!

It is a good idea to provide little bags for your guests to put their prizes into, especially if you are trying to cope with a lot of children – a lost prize is a major drama! You can either simply write each child's name on an ordinary paper bag or you could carry on your party theme by decorating a piece of card with, for instance, a pair of animals for a Noah's Ark party, printing the child's name on this, and stapling the card to your bag. An industrious and talented friend even made individual tiny carrier bags for each of her guests – needless to say the children were delighted.

It is a real bonus to have a children's party outside – thus avoiding any disturbance in your house – but it is always worth being prepared for rain. Plan sufficient games that can be played both indoors and outdoors, and have a room indoors cleared of furniture in case of need.

Indoor games for younger children

Grandmother's Footsteps

A suitable game to play when the children are arriving, with an adult as grandmother. This is the sort of game that children can join in at any stage of the proceedings. Ask the mothers to join in with their children to help break the ice. The 'grandmother' turns her back, and the children try to creep up on her from behind. Grandmother will, every now and again, suddenly turn around and if she sees anyone move they have to go back to the starting point.

Props: None.

'What's the time, Mr Wolf?'

'Mr Wolf' stands well in front of a line of children – with his back to them – as in Grandmother's Footsteps. The children creep up saying 'What's the time, Mr Wolf?'. He turns around to reply – '12 o'clock' – and if he sees anyone moving they have to go back to 'the House', ie, where they started from. At some point he replies 'Dinner time' and then tries to catch a child who is then Mr Wolf, and the game starts again. This is a good game to get the children shouting and joining in together.

Props: None.

Oranges and Lemons

The mothers form an arch and the children run in a line under the arch singing 'Oranges and lemons'. When they get to the 'chopping stage', whoever is chopped is out, until the last one is the winner. Here are the words:

> Oranges and lemons,
> say the bells of St Clements.
> You owe me five farthings,
> say the bells of St Martins.
> When will you pay me?
> say the bells of Old Bailey.
> When I grow rich,
> say the bells of Shoreditch.
> When will that be?
> say the bells of Stepney.
> I do not know,
> says the great bell of Bow.
>
> Here comes a candle
> to light you to bed.
> Here comes a chopper
> to chop off your head.
>
> Chop chop chop chop.

Why not end off with a 'tug of war' between the oranges and lemons? As each child is out they become an orange or lemon. At the end of the game the two teams have a good 'tug'! Any excuse for everyone to land on the floor!

Props: None.

'Simon Says'

One person stands in front of the rest as Simon. He faces them and calls out 'Simon says' (for example), 'put your hand on your head', and the children obey. But if he simply states 'Put your hand on your head' without the words 'Simon says...', then anyone who does it is out.
Props: None.

Musical Bumps

This is another excellent game to have before tea, to allow children to get rid of some excess energy. Have a practice run-through first. The children jump up and down to the music. When the music stops, they have to sit on the floor. Whoever sits down last is out, until eventually the winner is the last one left in.
Props: Music.

The Farmer's in his Den

The children stand in a circle with the mothers. Choose a farmer to be in his den. Then walk in a circle around the farmer singing 'The farmer's in his den', as the farmer chooses his wife, the wife a child and so on. When it comes to patting the 'bone', the last child to be chosen, make sure this is a gentle patting, and not an all-out-attack! For forgetful oldies the rhyme is as follows:

> The farmer's in his den
> The farmer's in his den
> Ee i diddily i
> The farmer's in his den.
>
> The farmer wants a wife
> The farmer wants a wife
> Ee i diddily i
> The farmer wants a wife.
>
> The wife wants a child
> The wife wants a child
> Ee i diddily i
> The wife wants a child.

Thereafter 'The child wants a nurse', 'The nurse wants a dog', 'The dog wants a bone', finishing off with 'We all pat the bone'.
Props: None.

Ring a Ring of Roses

The children hold hands and dance in a ring singing the words, then at 'we all fall down', they all fall down, usually roaring with laughter. Young children love this. Play this before sitting down to tea. Here are the words:

> Ring a ring of roses
> A pocket full of posies
> A-tishoo, A-tishoo
> We all fall down.

Props: None.

Pig, Sheep, Cow and Horse

Have a large picture of each of these animals and place them in each of the four corners of a room. Have the music playing and when it stops the children rush to whichever corner they choose. Some helper with their back turned calls out the name of one of the animals, and those in that particular corner are out. Continue until you find the winner.
Props: Four, if possible large, pictures of each of the animals; music.

Old Macdonald had a Farm

If you have a record for this, play it, and encourage the children to join in with all the animal noises. Or, if you are brave enough to sing it yourself, the words are as follows:

> Old Macdonald had a farm
> Ee i Ee i o
> Old Macdonald had a farm
> Ee i Ee i o
>
> And on that farm he had some hens
> Ee i Ee i o
> with a cluck cluck here
> and a cluck cluck there
> Here a cluck there a cluck
> everywhere a cluck cluck
> Old Macdonald had a farm
> Ee i Ee i o

Continue each verse with a different animal, but all the animal noises should be repeated in turn, in each verse, so that the verse gets longer and longer (perhaps give a prize to the child who can remember all the noises best?).
Props: None

Pass the Parcel

This is the best game to have after tea. Remember to prepare the parcel before the party. Choose a prize and then wrap it up – newspaper is fine – and then wrap this parcel in another layer of paper with a small present (for instance, a small wrapped sweet, not a large toffee) inside each layer, and continue wrapping layers with small presents, until you have allowed a layer for each child to unwrap Make sure that your maths is right! The children sit in a circle and pass the parcel from child to child, while the music is playing. Stop the music at intervals, and whoever is holding the parcel at that time, unwraps a layer. Each child should have a sweet, or whatever, by the end. Finally the last one is the main prize winner. Make sure that the host does not win the main prize.
Props: One small prize for last turn of game. Sufficient sheets of old wrapping or newspaper, and little sweet in between each layer to give each child a go; music.

Hunt the Thimble, Easter Eggs, or Sweets, etc

Another good game to play after tea. You can either play this so that there is only one prize, and whoever finds the thimble or the Easter egg, etc, wins, or you could have a little Easter egg or sweet for each child to find. Be careful that whichever way you play this game, the things are not hidden too near a fire, too high up, or near precious ornaments. For small children make the hiding places very easy. Once again, allow mums to help.
Props: Thimble, Easter eggs or sweets, whichever you decide to use.

Musical Cushions

Having had a less energetic game, Musical Cushions (or Bumps again) can let off a bit of energy. Have one less cushion than the number of children. The guests walk, dance, jump or whatever you want around the cushions to music. When the music stops,

everyone has to find a cushion to sit on, and whoever does not is out. Remove one cushion and start the music again. Repeat this until one cushion is left, with two children contesting for it. When the children are tiny they may want their mothers to do this with them.
Props: One cushion per guest; music.

Musical Hats

Substitute hats for the cushions, though they're obviously not to sit on! Have one less hat than the number of children. The guests walk, dance or jump around the hats to music, and when the music stops, everyone has to find a hat to put on, and whoever does not is out. Continue as above, removing a hat each time the music starts again, until only one hat is left with two children contesting for it.
Props: One hat per guest, music.

Musical Newspapers

A good substitute for Musical Cushions as you may not have many cushions – a husband who shall be nameless tried to organize this game and forgot the need for twenty props! Cut about 1 foot (30 cm) square of newspaper per child, and the children have to jump on them.
Props: One newspaper per guest; music.

Here we go round the Mulberry Bush

The children join hands and dance in a circle miming the actions of each verse in turn. Here are some verses to show the structure of the song:

Here we go round the mulberry bush
The mulberry bush the mulberry bush
Here we go round the mulberry bush
On a cold and frosty morning.

This is the way we wash our hands
Wash our hands wash our hands
This is the way we wash our hands
On a cold and frosty morning.

Other verses are – 'This is the way we clean our teeth', 'This is the way we brush our hair', 'This is the way we eat our tea' and 'This is the way we jump for joy'. And so on.
Props: None.

'Hokey Kokey'

Mothers will have to help. Everyone stands in a circle and you all sing:

You put your left arm in, left arm out,
Left arm in and you shake it all about.
You do the Hokey Kokey and you turn around,
That's what it's all about!

Ooh the Hokey Kokey (all hold hands and go in to the centre of the circle and out again, throughout the chorus),
Ooh the Hokey Kokey, Ooh the Hokey Kokey,
Knees bend, arms stretch, ra, ra, ra.

Remember that you put your arms, legs, feet, etc, in!
Props: None.

Pinning the Tail on the Donkey

The donkey can be the conventional animal, on to which you pin your tail, but if your party is a pirate party for instance, then use a treasure map on which the treasure trove is to be found. Draw the outline on to a stiff card, or a piece of paper pinned to a board. You might be able to find a suitable picture on a poster or a piece of wrapping paper. (Or you can buy the donkey and the tails from some large stationers.) Then make a separate tail either using paper, raffia, string or wool. Place the picture against the wall and mark on it the position where the tail should be. Blindfold one child at a time, give them the tail through which there is a drawing pin, and whoever places the tail on the paper nearest to the correct position is the winner. Initial each attempt. Some little children do not like the thought of a blindfold, so don't force the shy ones – they have just as much fun watching. Let them say with you who they think is the winner.

Props: Card or paper pinned to board as donkey, or whatever symbol you plan to use. A pin with the tail, cross, etc. A blindfold. Pencil for initialling.

Shopping

This is a good game to end your party with, but it does need preparation beforehand. Wrap up little parcels of Smarties, chocolate buttons, Refreshers, Dolly Mixtures, etc, in cling film. If you have the time and inclination tie with a little ribbon. Any small objects can be used – rubbers, little pencils, whatever you wish. Have a bag with lots of either pennies or toy or real money (you can get bags of pennies from banks, but if using real money, be careful that

the children are not too young and try to eat it). 'Hide' the money around your house, wherever you want, and let the children go and find the money and come to 'buy' either the little packets of sweets, or toys. These can be considered their going-home presents. Allow enough time for the children to have a proper game before their parents arrive.

Props: A bag of pennies, or toy money, little presents; some sort of stall from which you can 'sell' these to the children.

In-Between Games

Here are a few ideas to keep the children who are 'out' occupied until the next game. Sometimes when children are very little you won't need to do anything, as they will be quite happy just watching their friends. If you have sufficient room, have lots of toys out for them to play with, but if space is a problem, and if you can have an extra pair of hands to help, then why not use another room, and have some other activity going on in there. For example, have a jar or bowl of Smarties, or pennies, and get the guests to guess how many there are in the jar. Whoever wins can have a little prize. Your helper will need a pencil and paper to write down the names and number the child guessed.

Alternatively, have a box of straws and some Smarties in a bowl or plate. The children have to suck the Smarties with a straw on to another plate and they can eat the proceeds! If you have enough space, little children love playing Musical Bumps. While you have a musical game going on, have an 'out' section, who can jump around and do the bumps just for fun when the music stops, but it is important to keep those playing the proper game and those that are just having fun separate. You will need space.

Outdoor games for younger children

Don't forget that conventional indoor games can perfectly well be played outside – Musical Bumps, Hats, etc, Pass the Parcel, Pig, Sheep, Cow and Horse, etc. Also don't try to keep the younger children running all the time: they are only tiny, so have a Pass the Parcel for a rest. Have plenty of orange squash outside, as they'll be thirsty. If you are short of unbreakable beakers, collect up well ahead of the party, either small yogurt or cream pots, or washing powder measure mugs. Wash these thoroughly and they will be fine.

Running Races

Little ones have fun just running races and mums can join in! If you have a small garden have people running to the end and back.
Props: Washing line, if possible, for start and finish lines.

Egg and Spoon Race

Give each child a dessertspoon with a small potato in it. Whoever crosses the line first with the potato still in the spoon is the winner. If you are being firm, or if the children are old enough to understand, they ought perhaps to either go back to the beginning and start again when they drop the potato, or turn a circle.
Props: A dessertspoon and small potato per child.

Dressing-up Race

Have the children run to individual heaps of dressing-up clothes. They get dressed and run back.
Props: Lots of old scarves, hats, etc. One per guest. If you haven't many such clothes, run heats of four children, say, and then have a 'final'.

Relay Race

Divide the children into two teams. The first one in each team runs to a marker and round back to their team. The second child takes the baton, and this is repeated until the first team to finish wins. NB, when dividing the teams, try and make them evenly balanced.
Props: 2 batons (a piece of smooth wood); 2 markers (tall bamboo sticks, for instance).

Pitch and Chuck

Divide your guests into two teams. Have the children run to a ping pong ball and throw the ball into a bowl or paddling pool full of water. When they are tiny they may need some help with their aim, and also have the bowls or pools quite close to the balls. They run back and the next child then goes. Meanwhile a helper has retrieved the ball from the water. First team to finish wins.
Props: 2 washing-up bowls filled with water, or 1 paddling pool; 2 ping pong balls.

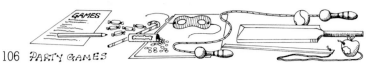

Buckets and Balloons

Divide your guests into teams. The first child runs to the bucket and picks up a balloon from inside. They run back to the next child and hand over the balloon. The next child runs to the bucket and puts the balloon back into it. Continue this until everyone has had a go. The first team to finish wins. Have a helper at the bucket end.

Props: 2 balloons, 2 spares and don't make the balloons too big or it will be hard to get them out of the bucket; 2 buckets.

Prince Charles, Princess Diana and their carriage

If you have twelve guests divide into three groups of four. From each group choose a Prince Charles, a Princess Diana and two horses. Have 'Prince Charles' at one end of the garden with a pile of his clothes, and put 'Princess Diana' at the other end with her clothes. Have the two horses with their skipping rope 'reins' in the middle. When the off is given, Prince Charles and Princess Diana get dressed. Prince Charles, when ready, runs to pick up his horses, puts the skipping rope around them and drives them to Princess Diana. She and Prince Charles then both drive the horses back to the start.

Props: Clothes for Charles and Diana and skipping ropes.

Sandpit, etc

If you are having an outdoor party a sandpit will enable the children to amuse themselves for quite a while. Have plenty of other outside toys – a tricycle, playhouse made out of travelling rugs on clothes airer, truck, rope ladder, swing, slide, play tunnel, etc. If the weather is really fine and there are plenty of mothers to help, have lots of towels and the paddling pool out. Have old washing-up liquid containers, plastic cups, etc, for them to play with in the water.

Prizes and Presents

Why not make a lollipop tree, by hanging lollies (or any little toys) on to a little bush or tree and the children could either collect prizes for games from it, or their presents at going-home time. All you need to do is tie pieces of cotton in loops from the presents, and suspend them from the tree.

Indoor games for older children

Some of the earlier games are obviously just as suitable for older children, so don't neglect the old favourites of Pass the Parcel, etc.

Pairing

Once mothers no longer stay during the party you may wish to encourage shy children to gain confidence by having a pairing game at the beginning of the party. If the children are too young to read, make cut-out recognizable shapes. If you are having a zoo or Noah's Ark party, for example, make animal shapes (if you are not good enough at drawing trace from a book), and remember to cut out two of each. When a child arrives, pin one to his or her chest, and the other on to another child's chest. Then they can all go around and find their partner. Later they can go into tea two by two, especially if it is a Noah's Ark party. Older children can have photographs of famous pairs of personalities, for instance Starsky to pair with Hutch, or Tom with Jerry. Or you can draw on a piece of paper or cut out of magazines, matching objects and pin one to each child – for instance, a tennis racquet and a tennis ball, a bird and a nest, and so on. If it is a *Star Wars* party, use space scenes in your pairing. Having divided the children up like this, you can also use the same pairing to create teams, with half of each pair in opposing teams, or you can let them play games in pairs, as in the next game and the tray game.

Props: Some badge or marker per child (sticky labels for instance), designed as you want.

Hunt the Pennies

Buy £1 or £2 worth of pennies from the bank, and hide these around the house. When the children come, they can rush around finding the pennies, come back to you and be given Smarties as a prize. This is a very good game to start the party with, while everyone is arriving.

Props: Sufficient pennies and Smarties for your guests.

Guess what or who they are

Pin photographs of famous people or objects around the room. Give each guest a piece of paper and a pencil and let them guess what or who the photographs are of. This is a game which could be done in pairs, especially if there are shy children.

Props: Photographs from magazines or newspapers; Blu-tack; pencil and paper per guest or pair.

Musical Knees

This is an ideal game for using your pairs, but only suitable for older children, who can support the weight of their partner. Dance in pairs. When the music stops one child has to sit on the other's knee. Those who move are out.

Props: Music.

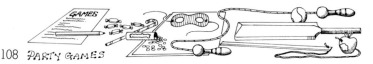
Tray Game

This is an ideal game for playing after tea, especially if the children have outgrown Pass the Parcel. Before the party place about twelve objects on a tray. Select your objects and the number according to the age group you are catering for. Use objects such as spoons, combs, pencils, and so on, that the children will be familiar with. This game can be played in pairs if the children are younger and need reassurance, or individually. Let the children look at the tray for a few minutes, then remove it, and give the children five minutes to write down the names of all the objects they can remember. Collect in the papers, and whoever has remembered the greatest number of objects is the winner. Be prepared for a few ties here, and have enough presents for more than one winner.

Props: 12 different objects; tea towel to conceal objects from prying eyes; tray; pencil and paper per guest or pair.

Musical Islands

Place pieces of newspaper on the floor, and have one less than the number of players. Let the children dance around to the music. When the music stops everyone has to find an island and stand on it with one foot and one hand and whoever cannot keep still is out. Don't expect the children to stay still for long. Remove one (or however many are out) island from the sea, and start the music again. Continue until one island is left, and two people are also left. The winner is whoever claims the last island first and balances there.

Props: Newspaper pieces 2 feet (60 cm) square per guest; music.

Musical Chairs

Substitute chairs for cushions (page 102).
Props: Chair per guest; music.

Musical Statues

The children dance around and when the music stops, they have to keep very still. Whoever moves is out.
Props: Music.

Also see Musical Bumps, etc, in section for younger children.

Treasure Hunt

Children usually find it more enjoyable to play this game in pairs. Make your preparations in advance, and have a certain amount of supervision in the house. Don't play it at all unless you are prepared for the whole house to be used during the game. Write out ten cards giving the names of different parts of the house, or pieces of furniture. A typical set of cards might read:

Upstairs mirror
Under cushion
Around tap
Behind radiator
Under upturned bucket
Under bed
Under chair
In atlas or large book (but sticking out)
Under rug
Behind curtain

Then write out ten (depending on the numbers of pairs of children) pieces of paper with the figure 1 on them, then ten with 2 on, and so on up to the number 10. (This is a job your children can do, but don't let them help with the hiding.) Keep one clue back and hide all the others in the appropriate places, together with the numbered slips of paper, all the 1's with the first clue, 2's with the second and so on. The last hiding place contains the last set of numbered pieces of paper and a little pile of wrapped sweets – one for each child. When the game begins, read out the first clue. Each pair of children then finds the first hiding place, and reads the next clue, but before looking for it, brings back one of the number 1 pieces of paper to you (this is to prove they are following the treasure hunt in the right order and to keep a check on their progress, in case some of the children need help). You then send them off to the next clue and so on, until they all finally reach the treasure, which is the pile of sweets. You can, if you like, also give a prize to the pair of children who finish the treasure hunt first.

Props: Enough cards (PC's or ordinary paper) per child or pair and same number of pieces marked 1, 2, 3 etc. Sweets.

Button Hunt

An adaptation of the Treasure Hunt. Divide the children into two teams, and let each team choose a captain, or if you have already paired the children, divide the two halves of each pair into two teams, and then let them choose the captain. Place the buttons around the house or, if you are having an outdoors party, around the garden before the children arrive. If the children are older, and you want to make the game more difficult, camouflage the buttons on a similar coloured background, for instance a brown button on a brown table. Then tell one team to shout 'Miaow' when they find a button, and the other team to shout

'Woof' when they do. The captain of each team is the only one allowed to pick the buttons up, as the buttons must not be touched by any team member, so be prepared for a lot of noise. If it is taking a long time to find the buttons, set a time limit of say, three minutes, and then the captain who has collected the most buttons represents the winning team.

Props: Lots of buttons.

Blindfold Smelling

Before the party prepare saucers of chocolate, tomato ketchup, coffee, orange, curry powder, and whatever else you like. Bring the children individually into the room, blindfolded, to see who can identify the most number of smells. Then, when they have had their go, let them sit and watch the others. But they must not call out the answers. This can also be done as a tasting game, or you can let the children both taste and smell. An alternative to this game is to blindfold the guests and then give them a pair of gloves to wear, and a selection of items to feel and identify. Whoever identifies the most is the winner.

Props: Saucers and 'smells'; blindfold; or objects to feel and gloves; or things to taste.

Sardines

Choose one person to go and hide, the rest then count to twenty, and go and search for the missing guest. This can be done in the dark (especially if older children are playing). When anyone finds the missing guest they join him very quietly and wait until everyone else has found the hiding place. The last person to find the tin of 'sardines' has to do a forfeit.

Props: None.

Railway Carriages

Before the party take one newspaper per guest, and muddle up all the pages. Then sit the children in a circle and give each one a jumbled newspaper. The first child to put the paper back into the correct order is the winner. Remember not to use varying sizes of newspapers, because the smaller ones are obviously going to be easier to handle.

Props: Collect enough copies of the same newspaper as number of guests (then they will all have the same size paper to cope with).

Pass the Balloon

Divide the children into two teams. Give each team leader a balloon. The team leader puts the balloon between his knees, and passes it down to the next person in the line, and so on. The team which does this most quickly is the winner.

Props: 2 balloons – 2 spares or more!

Pass the Matchbox

Divide the children into two teams. Give the captain of the team a matchbox cover. The children have to pass the matchbox on their noses along the line, without using their hands. Whichever team finishes first is the winner.

Props: 2 matchbox covers.

Pass the Orange

Divide the children into two teams. Give each captain an orange. He or she puts it under their chin and passes it down the line. A variation of this is for the two teams to lie on the floor and to pass the orange between their ankles.

Props: 2 oranges.

Balloon Running

Divide the children into two teams. Another way of playing passing the balloon if you have enough space, is to have the children running down the room and back with the balloons between their knees, and then passing it to the next member of the team. Whichever team finishes first is the winner.

Props: 2 balloons and spares.

Making Masks

Before the party, make basic masks out of coloured paper, and cut eye holes and mouth holes (see page 22). Attach strings. Have a supply of glue-on bought coloured shapes, and a large supply of felt-tip pens, and allow the children a certain length of time to make their own masks, decorating them with the coloured shapes and the felt-tips. Make sure that this is not done where felt-tips can harm either the children's clothes, or a table cloth, etc, and then let them all run around in their masks, and give a prize to the most imaginative.

Props: Masks; hole reinforcers; coloured shapes; felt-tips; string, etc.

Funny Hats

Provide each child with a large piece of coloured paper, newspaper, ribbon, pins, paperclips, and some odd bits of coloured tissue paper, and give them a certain length of time in which they have to make a hat. Whoever has the best product at the end is the winner.

Props: Paper; newspaper; paper clips; staples; pins; coloured tissue; shapes (ready glued).

Charades

Divide your guests into two teams. Give each team a list of suitable subjects – book or film titles, etc – and a few minutes to think about them. Then each team acts them to the other team, within a set time limit. Whichever team guesses the most titles is the winner. Doing it in teams avoids the embarrassment of individual people having to act the charades.
Props: None.

Apple Bobbing

A very suitable game for a Hallowe'en party. Play this game in the kitchen, or outside if the party is in the summer. Place a large bowl of water on the floor and float some apples in it. The guests kneel down with their hands behind their backs, and pick up the apples with their teeth. If your bowl is large enough you can have more than one person kneeling beside the bowl at a time. See who can pick out the most apples within a particular time limit.
Props: Large bowl; apples; something water resistant to put bowl on (a PVC cloth); towel to wipe faces.

Apple Variation

Using a skewer, pierce the apple through the core and thread a piece of string through the hole. Knot at the bottom and attach the string to a pole (eg, a broom handle balanced between two chairs). The children kneel down, with their hands behind their backs, and see which of them can eat an apple first. This may also be played using rolls or doughnuts, instead of apples. Push a skewer through the centre of the roll or bun, and thread the string through, tying the end of the string back on the broom handle.
Props: Broom stick; string; apples; skewer or similar. Poultry or upholstery needle for threading string.

Smarties in a Dish

Place some Smarties in a large bowl, give each guest a straw and a small plate. Have a time limit. The idea is for them to transfer the Smarties from the bowl to the plate without using their hands, by sucking the Smarties up one at a time, at the end of the straw. Whoever has the most Smarties on their plate at the end of the time limit is the winner. A less expensive version of this game can be played with dried peas or beans.
Props: Smarties, dish; straws; plates.

Jar of Smarties

Place a certain number of Smarties or other sweets in a glass jar before the party. The children have to guess how many Smarties are in the jar, and whoever guesses the nearest to the correct number wins the Smarties.
Props: Lots of Smarties (you can buy giant tubes); jar; pencil and paper to list names and guesses.

Shopping List

Sit the children in a ring. The first child says, 'I went shopping and I bought . . . a cabbage.' Number two says, 'I went shopping and I bought a cabbage and some toothpaste.' Number three adds to the list until someone forgets the correct list, and they are out. The game continues until a winner is found.
Props: None.

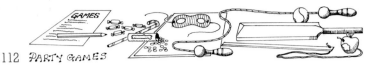

Bun Fight (not really!)

Take a long piece of string or garden twine and a piece per guest of a smaller length of string. Allow half a currant bun per guest, and make a hole in each half. Thread the buns with the short pieces of string and knot underneath. Then tie each of these pieces, leaving about 1 foot (30 cm) between, to the long string. Two helpers hold either end of the long string, and the children try to eat the buns as they dangle there. The helpers can jerk the string about a little while the guests are trying to eat.

Props: Long piece of string or garden twine; small pieces of similar; half currant bun per guest; 2 helpers.

Shoeing the Horse

Divide the children into two teams. Place a chair in front of each team, and by it four washing powder measuring cups. Blindfold one member of each team, who then has to try to put the cups underneath the legs of the chair. Each member of the teams has to do this, and the first team to finish is the winner.

Props: 8 washing powder cups, or similar; 2 chairs (NB, with legs that will fit in the cups); 2 blindfolds. Have plenty of extra cups in case any get broken.

Jigsaw Game

Allow three Christmas cards per guest. Cut each card into four pieces, and keep one piece of each card back, but hide the rest around the house. The children are then given the piece you hold, to find its lost parts. Once they have found one complete card, give them another single piece and repeat. Whoever gets most cards wins the game.

Props: Old Christmas cards.

Around the World

Using about fifteen place names, have pieces of paper around the room, with different cities or countries in the world written on each piece. Have one 'Home'. Each guest is given a list containing the names of these places, but each list is written in a different order. The children start from Home and have to run to each place according to the order on their list. When they go to each place, they tick that one off. The first child to complete the list and run Home wins.

Props: 15 place names; Blu-tack; a list of the names for each child (NB, in different orders); pencil per guest.

Pass the Parcel with Forfeits

Have a list of forfeits, one per person. Wrap up the parcel with as many sheets of paper as there are guests (but without sweets between the layers). When the music stops, whoever is holding the parcel has to perform a forfeit – kiss his or her neighbour, do a head stand, hop around the circle on the outside, eat a biscuit in one minute, say your eight times table (do be kind though – it's agony if your mind goes blank), sing a song.

Props: 1 parcel wrapped in many layers of paper; list of forfeits; music.

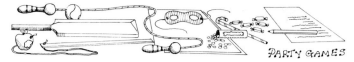

Team Tickles

Divide your guests into two teams. Have two very long pieces of string (the length depends on the number of your guests) with a dessertspoon tied to the end of each piece. The first team member has to 'thread' the spoon through their clothes, downwards, and pass the spoon to the next member, who threads it through their clothes upwards. NB, the first person has to hold on to the end of the piece of string so that it doesn't get pulled through and out. The first team to sit down, all joined together, is the winner.

Props: 2 very long pieces of string; 2 dessertspoons.

Hearts, Diamonds, Clubs, Spades

Each corner of the room is named by a card from each suit. Play some music and everyone must run around the room to the music. When the music stops, the children run to any corner that they choose. An organizer cuts a pack of cards and if a heart, for instance, is turned up, then the children in that corner are disqualified. Continue until a winner is found.

Props: Blu-tack; a pack of cards; music.

Chocolate Chopping

Children sit in a circle. Place in the centre one large bar of chocolate, on a plate, with a knife and fork. Also place by them a pair of gloves, a hat and scarf. The guests throw a dice (one turn each). Whoever throws a six rushes to put on the clothes and attempts to chop and eat some of the chocolate with the knife and fork. This operation must take place before another six is thrown, otherwise the turn is forfeit and the clothes are grabbed by the next child in an attempt to chop the chocolate.

Props: 2 large bars of chocolate (unwrapped); plate; knife and fork; hat; scarf; 1 pair of gloves.

In-between Games

We hope that you will have sufficient games here not to have children hanging around and getting bored, and waiting for the next game to start. However, when the children are 'out', here are some thoughts for games to keep them amused, until the main game has finished. Have plenty of Pocketeers on the side – pocket games, electronic games if you have them. A game of Bagatelle or table football is always popular, so long as you have sufficient room. There is a very amusing game you can buy called Twisters which any number can play. Again you need space. If you have sufficient help, as we suggested for the younger children, perhaps someone could be organizing the straw and Smartie game, or guessing the Smarties in a jar (page 111).

Outdoor games for older children

The former games can of course be played outside, but the following are specifically for outdoor parties. For most of these games you need either 2 long pieces of garden twine, string, or washing line as start and finish lines.

Boys' Adventure Dash or Assault Course

This is a very good game for energetic chaps to play before tea. It needs to be prepared before the party, and will depend very much on the size and shape of your garden, and also on the play equipment you can provide. Prepare a course with about ten obstacles to be tackled. You could either play this as a team event, having two identical courses, and whichever team completes the course first in the right order wins; or using a stop watch, time each individual child and whoever is fastest wins. Have a few adults around in case any of the children get into difficulties. Here are some suggestions for the course:

1. Throw a ball into a bucket. (2 balls; 2 buckets)

2. Climb through a tyre (hanging up) or an open ended barrel. (2 tyres or barrels)

3. Score a goal. (2 balls; 2 goals made with 4 bean poles)

4. Run along a board, balanced on two lying-down tyres, or two bales of straw. (2 boards, straw or tyres)

5. High jump. (3 thin bean poles for each jump: and 2 clothes pegs. Attach pegs to 2 of poles to make 2 rests. Use third pole to lie across)

6. Long jump. (4 pieces twine or plastic covered line etc)

7. Jump a set distance in a sack, or with feet tied together with a duster. (2 dustbin liners or 2 dusters)

8. Run with an egg and spoon (potato and dessertspoon) a long or short distance, and back again to place the spoon ready for the next member of the team. If anyone drops the potato they have to start again.

9. If you have an assault course rope ladder, then up and down once.

10. Climb a rope ladder, and touch a specific point.

11. Stepping stones – place several bricks or breeze blocks in a line as stepping stones.

12. Dribble a ball around bending poles. (2 balls and several bean poles)

13. Run on stilts. You can buy mini stilts or make them yourself before the party. For each pair of stilts you will need two identical sized cocoa or other cans (do not use ones which have been opened by a can opener, in case of accidents with jagged edges); 2 pieces of thick string or washing line, each about 2 feet (60 cm) long; a skewer or similar piercing instrument. Make two holes on either side of each can, thread your string through the can and join it to make a large loop. The children can then balance on the can and use the loop part as the stilt.

14. A somersault at the finishing post.

Throwing the Wellie

You need a lot of space for this game. Have any number of old tyres or hoops, and number these 10, 4, 2, etc. The children throw the wellies from a starting line into the tyres or hoops. Whoever has the highest score wins.
Props: Markers for points; tyres/hoops etc; lots of boots; score sheet.

Matchbox Hunt

Let the children either play in pairs or as individuals. Give each child or pair a matchbox. Tell them to find as many things as they can fit into the matchbox in 2 minutes. Whoever collects most is the winner.
Props: 1 matchbox per guest or pair.

Pitch and Putt

This is a surprisingly difficult game, and suitable for older children only. Allow two children to have their turns together (or play as a team game). The children stand behind a line and chip golf balls into the following: a tyre, box, paddling pool, or a circle painted on the ground. Don't put these too far away. Each target must have a score marker by it, with different scores. Whoever gets the highest score wins. Allow one or two shots at each target. Children retrieve their balls after their turn and the next guest has a try.
Props: Golf balls and suitable clubs; targets and their score markers – old bamboo sticks slit with paper markers; score sheet and pencils; washing line for base line; short grass (that's not too precious!).

Shipwreck

Choose a child to be 'He'. The 'He' chases the other children who are only safe when off the ground, on straw bales, rugs, newspapers, etc, which serve as islands. If a child is touched by the 'He', while not on an island, then that guest takes over and chases the others. There is no real winner to this game, it can go on until you think the children have had enough.
Props: Depends on how you want to play the game.

Dressing-up Game

Before the party prepare two hats, two jackets or large shirts, two skirts or baggy trousers, and two pairs of grown-up size wellington boots. Divide the guests into two teams and have them queue up behind the starting line. For each team lay out, first, the hat, then a few yards further off the shirt, then the skirt or trousers ending up with the boots. Mark the end of the course with a stick or beanpole. The children have to run up one by one, put the clothes on, run around the end of the course marker, back again and take the clothes off in the opposite order, boots first, then the skirt or trousers, and finally the hat. Each member of the two teams does the same thing, and whichever team finishes first is the winner.
Props: Clothes as noted above.

Sack Race

Have one sack per guest, or use only two sacks, and divide the guests into two teams, making it into a team sack race.

Props: Sacks – if real sacks cannot be found, use dustbin liners (but they're not so durable).

Three-legged Race

Have plenty of large men's handkerchiefs or dusters, and pair the children off. Tie their inside legs together.

Props: Hanky or duster per pair of guests.

Wheelbarrow Race

Play this game before tea, or not until well after tea. Again pair the children off. One acts as the wheelbarrow, walking on his or her hands, and one as the 'pusher', holding the 'wheelbarrow's' legs.

Props: None.

Tug of War

This is particularly good fun when you have a tug of war between boys and girls. You can mark a line over which one team has to pull the other to win, but usually it's just the energetic pulling that's appreciated! Use a washing line for the rope.

Props: Washing line.

Slow Bicycle Race

Divide the guests into two teams. Each team needs a bicycle. Individual members of the team bike to a certain point in the garden and back, as slowly as possible. The team to finish last wins.

Props: 2 bicycles; 2 markers.

Balloon Race

Allow two blown up balloons per child, and slip an elastic band securely round the knot so it forms a loop. Children attach a balloon to each ankle with the elastic band. When the whistle blows they race to the winning line – without falling over or bursting their balloons.

Props: Two balloons per child; elastic bands.

French Cricket

There is no winner with this game, but children enjoy playing it. Someone stands with either a tennis racket or a cricket bat. Using a tennis ball the other children try to get the batsman out, by hitting his legs below the knees. If the batsman hits the ball he can turn to face the way the ball will be coming back at him. If however he has missed it, he is not allowed to do this.

Props: Always use a soft tennis ball; a tennis racquet or cricket bat.

It's a Knock Out

(Girls' version of the assault course, page 114). The course needs to be prepared before the party, and as with the assault course will depend very much on the size of your garden, and the equipment you can provide. Play this as a two-team event. Here are some ideas for the course:

1. Throw tennis ball into bucket.
2. Climb through a tyre.
3. High jump.
4. Long jump.
5. Sack jumping (a dustbin liner).
6. Dressing up in huge wellington boots, a skirt and a hat, then getting on stilts in fancy dress.
7. Stepping stones in fancy dress.
8. Ping pong balls into plate, in fancy dress. They have to suck with a straw to lift a ping pong ball on to a plate.
9. 5 skips in fancy dress, with skipping rope.
10. Undress, run back to team, with egg and spoon.

Props: See page 114 for stilts and stepping stones; 2 pairs of wellingtons (large); clothes, etc; tennis balls; buckets; tyres; etc.

Garden Hunt

This is an outdoor version of the Treasure Hunt (page 108). Prepare and play it in the same way, the only difference being that as cards or pieces of paper are likely to blow away out of doors, you should make sure that the clue cards are firmly secured (to a branch, under a pot, etc) and, instead of numbered cards, use lengths of different coloured thread, wool or string (red for the first clue, blue for the second and so on), which the children bring back to you. Suggestions for clues:

In sand pit
Around garden tap
Under bucket
Beside bicycle
Under flower pot
On branch of tree
Under greenhouse door
Under stone
Under garden seat
Beside steps

Props: Pieces of wool; cards etc.

5. OTHER PARTY IDEAS

If you want a change from the conventional tea party, give either a lunch, barbecue, picnic, high tea or supper party instead. You can have these in tandem with treats for older children – visits to the theatre, films, seaside or a conjurer at home. Whether you want large or smaller numbers of guests these parties will be great fun, and at the end of this section we give ideas on appropriate types of food.

Barbecues

If you have a portable or in-built barbecue in your garden this is an ideal way to entertain older children in the summer – children love to eat out of doors and barbecued food is wonderfully easy to cook and serve. Arrange to have at least two adults around – one to cook and one to supervise the children – and of course it goes without saying that none of the children should go near the lighted barbecue.

It is very important to light the barbecue at least one hour before you need to start the cooking as this will give the charcoal plenty of time to heat up so that the food will cook quickly without burning. The flames should have died down leaving a mass of red embers before you start the cooking. There is nothing worse than chicken drumsticks or sausages that are raw in the middle, unless it is hungry children standing around while you prod the food! It is quite acceptable to use a firelighter

to light the barbecue, but again be sure to allow plenty of time for the smell to wear off. Just before you start the cooking sprinkle some fresh or dried herbs or a spray of sage or rosemary over the charcoal – this smells delicious and gives the meat a lovely flavour. You can pre-cook the food indoors, earlier, and just finish off on the barbecue, especially if you are catering for larger numbers.

Food

Keep the food simple; in any case all food tastes twice as good when cooked out of doors. Have everything prepared in advance, so that you can get straight on with the cooking when the time comes. Aim to provide a selection of food so that each guest can have one or two or three of the following ideas. Cook some extra as well in case seconds are needed. Sausages, chicken drumsticks, beefburgers, spare ribs, small lamb chops, kebabs made of lamb or pork with mushrooms or sausage pieces in between the meat. Kebabs made with turkey meat are an excellent idea now that turkey is available in pieces. Brush oil over the meat before and during the cooking. Season the oil, if you like, with finely chopped herbs and salt and pepper. Many children like garlic, so if you decide to use it, press it through a garlic crusher and mix it with the oil before starting the cooking.

With the meat serve some simple salads

which you will have made before your guests arrive, small baked potatoes (to be cooked in your oven unless you have a very large barbecue and masses of time) or garlic, herb or peanut bread, prepared in advance, wrapped in foil and put in the oven 40 minutes before you plan to eat. Serve a simple barbecue sauce or just tomato sauce.

When it comes to puddings, again keep them simple and prepare them in advance. If your barbecue is a birthday party, then try one of the ice cream cakes on pages 73–75. Strawberries or raspberries when in season would be a special treat served with ice cream or a meringue. A simple fruit salad or ice cream served with Mars Bar sauce (page 120) would be a popular way to finish the meal – be prepared for lots of seconds.

Lunch, High Tea or Supper Parties

When your children reach the age of, say, eight and upwards you might find it more convenient to provide a meal other than a tea party. Perhaps you are planning a visit to a zoo, a pantomime or a cinema, and want to combine this with a meal that can be prepared in advance and served up quickly. In this case lunch or high tea is the best answer. Or, again, if you have older children who might dominate the little ones, then give a lunch party for the tinies while the others are at school, but remember to save some of the party food for when the older ones come home so that they won't feel left out. In this case it can be just as much of a party as a tea party if you organize games before and after the meal (see the games chapter) and use some of our ideas from the rest of this book on decorations, prizes, going-home presents and so on.

High tea is a simple meal to prepare and serve, and if you have been out on an expedition the children will probably want a rapid 'warm-up', so have everything prepared beforehand and the table set so that you won't be in a muddle on your return. If you decide on, for instance, a stew as a main course then you could leave this with jacket potatoes in a slow oven while you are out. Don't plan to have a meal that takes a long time to heat through on your return with the starving masses. Beefburgers in rolls or with oven chips are popular; so too are sandwiches made with a sandwich maker if you have one – add some chutney for extra flavour – but keep this for small numbers.

Use flapjacks, shortbread, etc, from the tea party food section, and leave on the tea table covered with cling film, but don't bother with ordinary sandwiches. If it has been a freezing afternoon, or early evening, some children may like hot chocolate to drink, but ask before preparing gallons as some do not like hot drinks. Otherwise, large 2 litre bottles of Coke and a soft alternative would be fine, or try a more adventurous drink (pages 95–97). Have a cake to fit in with your outing and having had a good warm through maybe an ice cream cake as a pudding would be fun – a Mars Bar sauce (page 120) served hot on the ice cream would make it even more delicious.

Whilst you are getting everything organized why not have the children playing some games – plan suitable ones beforehand – so that they are not around your feet.

When little girls are about eight, a real treat is to give a later party – say 5.30 to 8.00 pm, or if at a weekend, 7.30 in case parents are themselves wanting to go out – and make it a supper party instead of tea. It is best done in the winter, as darkness is important: a candle-lit dinner makes them feel extremely grown-

up! Above all else it is important that everything looks very pretty. Use paper plates and cups, etc, and keep a colour theme for your table: 'pink party' would be effective with pink candles, little posies of pink and white flowers (keep them tiny) on the table, pink paper napkins, pink and white streamers around the room etc. Keep everything dainty and small – to girls of this age, small is beautiful! Use tiny flowers, give tiny presents to go home – little scented rubbers or tiny little lavender bags you could make out of remnants. Have some games or perhaps a little home-made disco when the children arrive, followed by supper – which we found took them hours, they ate masses, and we were amazed! – and then you could have a conjurer or film show to end the evening off. This may sound as if it is a lot of work – it actually isn't and they love to feel sophisticated, some arriving in their long dresses. Whatever soft or fizzy drink, you serve, it must be called 'wine!'

Food

As far as food is concerned children like what they know, so keep it familiar. You don't want the party spoilt by your guests refusing to eat your food, but as it is a party make it just that bit more special and take extra care in preparing and serving it so that it looks both appetizing and attractive. Some of these ideas are more suitable for lunch-time parties, some are better for high teas or supper parties, but you can make your choice accordingly. Most of them can be prepared in advance, and need only last minute final touches.

First course

Shepherd's Pie – top with a layer of sliced or grated cheese to make a crunchy topping
Chicken and Mushroom Pies – to add a special touch why not make individual pies

Potato Moussaka – layers of cooked mince, sliced cooked potatoes, and cheese sauce
Savoury Pancakes – filled with chicken and ham in sauce
Grilled Gammon and Pineapple
Roast Chicken and Chipolatas – make it a roast turkey for large numbers
Chicken in Sauce – served with mashed potatoes piped round the edge of the dish
Turkey and Ham Croquettes
Spaghetti Bolognese
Beef Stew
Sausages in a Bacon Blanket – grill sausages, wrap rashers of streaky bacon round sausages, secure with a skewer or cocktail sticks, put under grill, turning once
Baked Potatoes – scoop out the insides, mash them with butter, cheese and chopped ham, and brown under the grill
Vols-au-vent.

Serve these with simple vegetables, for instance, oven chips, peas and baby carrots, coleslaw or a salad full of chopped dates, raisins, cubes of cheese, orange segments, hardboiled eggs, etc (children love lots of these).

Puddings

An ice cream cake – see pages 73–75. Make it in advance, keep in the freezer and take it out when required.
Apple Meringue – colour both the apple and the meringue pink
Fruit Salad in a melon basket
Pineapple – cut lengthways, served in its skin and decorated with glacé cherries
Chocolate Lemon Cups – see page 81
Chocolate, lemon or orange mousse
Ice cream and Mars Bar sauce – just chop Mars Bar into pan with a little water, and stir constantly over a gentle heat

Knickerbocker Glory
Cheesecake
Meringue Pavlova – filled with strawberries or raspberries and decorated with whipped cream
Mandarin and melon balls – this could also be a starter for the supper party.

Picnics

Organization is the key to a picnic party. If you are planning a visit to a castle, zoo or adventure park, check the opening times – and the open season! A trip to the seaside would be lovely, but don't go so far afield to make the day too long for all concerned. Plan to play a few games in the car and organize a few outdoor games to fill in any gaps, when you arrive at the destination. You cannot afford to leave things behind, and to avoid an irate husband, make a careful check list of all the food, drink and etceteras, you will need. Only ask numbers that can be seated comfortably. You can just take a party to the local park or woods for a picnic tea – it will save a lot of mess at home. Have sufficient helpers, especially if you are walking there, crossing roads clutching the picnic basket and a dozen little hands.

What To Take

Kitchen towels or paper napkins, damp J cloths in plastic bag; plastic bag for rubbish; basic first aid kit; Waspeze or insect repellant spray (incense sticks help too); sun tan cream; rugs to sit on; bottle opener (cork screw if required!); a spare set of children's clothes; ball, especially if taking boys; whistle to round up the troops. Collect these things in a washing-up bowl, which itself could be invaluable if someone feels carsick. Take a telephone number of a parent who could let others know if you are delayed and will be home late.

Food

The easiest way to give a picnic meal is to pack a 'nose bag' for each child. You may find bits of food are wasted but it takes all the hassle out of saving the 'bits and bobs' of a picnic. Collect up plastic margarine or ice cream ½ litre boxes or similar and pack each with the food.

For picnic, take (per child): lunch

Packet of crisps; cold chipolata sausage; cold chicken drumstick (you can buy frozen drumsticks in packs very reasonably); a few sticks of carrot and cucumber; small tomato if firm (but can be messy); small roll (buttered); small apple or banana; mini Mars or similar, or mini box of raisins. If you want to do a pudding, take in addition individual pots of yogurt or lemon mousse for each child in old yogurt pots and take plastic spoons. Simplest of all buy an ice cream each.

For tea

Two sandwiches (make two sorts and give one of each); flapjack; brownie; chipolata; sausage roll; packet of hula hoops; avoid melting chocolate biscuits and give a KP chocolate dip to each; if not taking a large birthday cake why not give each a separate cup cake (perhaps piped with the child's name); small apple; mini packet of Smarties, Twix, or similar.

As far as drinks are concerned take a flask of plain water (can be very handy if only to give the dog a drink); fizzy drinks can cause fizzy 'tums', so avoid in large quantities. Buy individual cans or cartons of juices plus straws. Take extra flasks of soft drinks and use old yogurt or cream pots for glasses.

Index